THE SPECIAL PROCEDURES OF THE HUMAN RIGHTS COUNCIL

THE SPECIAL PROCEDURES OF THE HUMAN RIGHTS COUNCIL

A brief look from the inside and perspectives from outside

Edited by Humberto Cantú Rivera

Foreword by Emmanuel Decaux

With contributions from
Navi Pillay
Olivier De Schutter
Magdalena Sepúlveda Carmona
Catarina de Albuquerque
Olivier de Frouville
Michael K. Addo
John H. Knox
Catalina Rivera Díaz
Minerva Martínez Garza

intersentia
Cambridge – Antwerp – Portland

Intersentia Ltd
Sheraton House | Castle Park
Cambridge | CB3 0AX | United Kingdom
Tel.: +44 1223 370 170 | Email: mail@intersentia.co.uk

Distribution for the UK:
NBN International
Airport Business Centre, 10 Thornbury Road
Plymouth, PL6 7 PP
United Kingdom
Tel.: +44 1752 202 301 | Fax: +44 1752 202 331
Email: orders@nbninternational.com

Distribution for the USA and Canada:
International Specialized Book Services
920 NE 58th Ave. Suite 300
Portland, OR 97213
USA
Tel.: +1 800 944 6190 (toll free)
Email: info@isbs.com

Distribution for Austria:
Neuer Wissenschaftlicher Verlag
Argentinierstraße 42/6
1040 Wien
Austria
Tel.: +43 1 535 61 03 24
Email: office@nwv.at

Distribution for other countries:
Intersentia Publishing nv
Groenstraat 31
2640 Mortsel
Belgium
Tel.: +32 3 680 15 50
Email: mail@intersentia.be

The Special Procedures of the Human Rights Council. A brief look from the inside and perspectives from outside
Humberto Cantú Rivera (ed.)

ISBN 978-1-78068-344-7
D/2015/7849/104
NUR 828

British Library Cataloguing in Publication Data. A catalogue record for this book is available from the British Library.

To Catalina, Humberto and Guillermo

ACKNOWLEDGEMENTS

There are many people who deserve to be acknowledged in these pages, for their time and their contribution to the realization of this book, but also for being a source of inspiration. First of all, I would like to acknowledge and thank Professor Emmanuel Decaux: his guidance, trust, patience, continuous support and sincere interest in my work have been an important part of my professional experience, and have greatly contributed to my deep interest and commitment to the defense and promotion of human rights. In addition, I would like to thank him for accepting to draft a foreword to this edited volume, and for doing so in quite an expeditious manner despite his many time constraints.

I must also thank several staff members working at the Office of the High Commissioner for Human Rights in Palais Wilson, those that most of the times perform their work relentlessly in the promotion, defense and standard-setting in the field of human rights, usually backstage. They were the source of many lessons learned, of camaraderie and teamwork, and of great moments in Geneva. My admiration and gratefulness to Mara Bustelo, Laure-Anne Courdesse, Leonardo Castilho, Ramin Pejan, Madoka Saki, Juana Sotomayor, Ulrik Halsteen, Orlagh McCann, Bárbara Mateo, Lidia Rabinovich, Boris Tchoumavi and Rebaone Ferguson, who were or continue to be part of the Sustainable Human Development Section of the Special Procedures Branch.

Of course, my deep gratefulness and appreciation also goes to all the mandate-holders appearing in this book, who graciously accepted my invitation and decided to dedicate several hours of their extremely packed schedule to the drafting and reviewing of the pages in this book, many of them in between Council sessions and during periods of extreme activity in the elaboration and presentation of reports to the Human Rights Council or General Assembly. I also want to specially thank Ms. Navi Pillay and her team, for agreeing to the interview that serves as an introductory note in this book, and for her encouraging words that she shared with me a couple of times in the halls of Palais Wilson.

My recognition also goes to the Human Rights Commission of Nuevo Leon in Monterrey, Mexico, for deciding to pursue this project with me in its original Spanish edition, and who have now extended their support to this English version. Both Minerva Martínez and Catalina Rivera have devoted many hours away of their particularly busy schedule in the defense of human rights at the local level; their contributions are particularly relevant and useful to add a local vision to the work undertaken at the international level by the Human Rights Council and its mandate-holders, as well as by Treaty Bodies and the Office of the High Commissioner.

Many others also deserve a special mention, at both the personal and professional levels: Philippe Armand de Bonneval, Javier Tous, Caio Valentim, Tara Sepehrifar, Claire Fenton-Glynn, Zorah Blok, Jessie Kerry, Orlymar García, Ingvil Sahr, María Sureda, Sanaz Sedigh, Juliette Hignard, Camille Couvert, Robyn Boosey, Chloe Vigneau-Ribal, Luisa Meneghetti, Kirsten Hommes, Andrés del Castillo, Pétalla Timo, Aline Vicentim, Elisa Muñoz, Sergii Masol, Inge Geraardyn, Catalina Catan and Quentin Rapaud. Special thanks also to Juan Manuel Iglesias, Pablo Contreras, Astrid Osorio, Juan Pablo Guerrero, Paula Arias, Carmen Crespo, Sarah Almeida and Ana María García Ceceña; Andreas Borgeas, Hans Schmitz, Robert Klotz, Miriam Heredia, Carolina Miró, Anaïs Schill, Thomas Gillot, Savani Gupte and Julie Baloup; to Stéphanie Gervais, Chris Kip, Jernej Cernic, Surya Deva, Gentian Zyberi, Santiago Ramírez Reyes, Rafael Ibarra Garza, Samantha Colli, Anna Glazewski, Audrey Lebret, Laurent Trigeaud, Catherine Kessedjian, Ana López Hechem, Amalia Muñoz, Keila Kraul, Walid Tijerina and Jorge Castillo. There are many others; some I cannot name.

I would also like to thank the CRDH of Université Panthéon-Assas, for providing me an academic shelter and a constant challenge, as well as many opportunities; the Governments of France and Mexico, for their financial support and interest in my professional project; and the School of Law and Criminology of the Universidad Autónoma de Nuevo León, my alma mater, and its two most recent Deans, who have graciously supported my work. Last but not least, I would like to thank Tom Scheirs and the team at Intersentia, for their patience and editorial support. Finally, heartfelt thanks to my family: Humberto, Catalina, Guillermo and Angie, I cannot find the appropriate words to thank you for being so patient in the long hours of work, and for pushing me to always keep working and not giving up.

FOREWORD

Emmanuel Decaux*

I am particularly happy that Mr. Humberto Cantú Rivera assembled the essays written by the best specialists in the field for this volume, previously published in Spanish and now translated to English. This work shows the dynamism of the Human Rights Commission of Nuevo Leon in the areas of awareness and research. On this note, this publication is timely and in line with the United Nations Declaration on Human Rights Education and Training, adopted by consensus by the General Assembly on 19 December 2011 following the work of a drafting group of the Advisory Committee of the Human Rights Council, where I had the honor of being the rapporteur. As it was recently recalled by the new High Commissioner Zeid al-Hussein, the successor of Navi Pillay, in his first intervention in the "High-Level Segment" of the March 2015 session of the Human Rights Council: "*The most powerful instrument in the arsenal we have against poverty and conflict is the weapon of massive instruction. Respect for human rights of all, justice, education, equality – these are the strongly interlocking elements that will build fair, confident and resilient societies; true development and a permanent peace.*"[1]

It is equally welcome that the last contribution in this volume is that of Ms. Minerva Martínez Garza, President of the Human Rights Commission of Nuevo Leon, dedicated to NHRI cooperation with the Special Procedures of the Human Rights Council. These independent national institutions, "third-type actors" between the branches of State and the lively force of civil society, have conquered their place in the United Nations system. We track their progress in the fifteen years since the adoption of the Paris Principles that took place in the Center for International Conferences in Avenue Kléber in 1991, and until the creation of the Human Rights Council and the establishment of the Universal Periodic Review in 2006. The diversity of

* Professor at Université Panthéon-Assas Paris II, and President of the UN Committee on Enforced Disappearances.

1 UN High Commissioner for Human Rights, *Opening speech to the High-Level Segment of the Human Rights Council* (02 March 2015).

NHRIs doesn't make collective solutions easy, but it would be useful that Treaty Bodies adopt a common approach while taking in consideration the specificities of their respective mandates. Thus, according to the criteria of the International Coordination Committee, only one "national institution" in each Member State can receive the "A Status" that guarantees full international recognition; however, this leaves provincial commissions or specialized institutions outside of their scope, regardless of their independent character or expertise, either in the areas of protection of children, on the fight against discrimination or on the inspection of detention sites. In this point, a certain degree of empiricism is necessary to avoid neglecting direct sources of information with profound field experience.

The concern of NHRIs being *victim-oriented* is attested by another contribution from a member of the Human Rights Commission of Nuevo Leon, that of Catalina Rivera Díaz, who targets communications and the special procedures. NHRIs can participate directly or indirectly in urgent appeals requested to special procedures, and *mutatis mutandis* to treaty bodies having similar competences, open to every person "having a legitimate interest", as is the case of NHRIs in accordance with their mandate. The question of their role as *amicus curiae* in communications procedures before treaty bodies is more complex, given that this procedure is written, confidential and adversarial. In other words, NHRIs can only intervene if they are briefed on a case by one of the two parties in the procedure, the State or the complainant, rendering them into a stakeholder more than an independent third party. It seems to me, however, that NHRIs are better suited to participate in matters related to the follow-up of statements made by conventional bodies. A fundamental concern of the different mandate-holders is the protection of victims and their relatives, as well as of human rights defenders, against every type or measure of intimidation or reprisals. In those cases, NHRIs, as well as OHCHR offices, have an irreplaceable role to play before the responsible State authorities.

An underlying question is the articulation of the levels of protection, not only at the domestic level – between the provincial and federal levels – but also in the international sphere, between the regional and universal systems. The legitimate attachment to the Inter-American System – as to the European or the more recent African systems – cannot be at the expense of the affirmation of universal principles or UN bodies. Thus, the affirmation of Mexico as a State governed by the rule of law and as a protector of human rights goes hand in hand with the acceptance of international procedures, including individual communications and inter-State complaints before the United Nations Treaty Bodies.

But the interest of this book is beyond the state of Nuevo Leon or even of Mexico, and I am sure that all readers will be seduced by the multiplicity and richness of perspectives on the dynamics of human rights. The creation of the Special Procedures took place during the occurrence of extreme experiences, such as the dictatorship of General Pinochet in Chile or the "Operation Condor" in Latin America, which provoked the establishment of the Working Group on Enforced or Involuntary Disappearances in 1980. Olivier de Frouville, its former Chair-Rapporteur, concentrates on the motor role of the Working Group in the progressive development of legal standards, with the adoption of the Declaration in 1992 by the General Assembly while the International Convention took form, which would enter into force twenty years later, in 2011. We must also recall the role undertaken by the Working Group on Arbitrary Detention, who under the impetus of Louis Joinet had itself a pioneering role.

The multiplication of thematic procedures, in parallel to the substantive work of the Treaty Bodies through their general comments, would lead the editor to make a choice. The introductory chapter by Humberto Cantú Rivera sets forth the collective logic of a system in perpetual movement, with its strengths and weaknesses, taking into account not only the personality of the mandate-holders, but also the precariousness of the "lease" accorded to them and which is sometimes challenged. The choices made are wise, even if the grand thematic procedures in the field of civil and political rights or of "public freedoms" are relatively eclipsed by the economic and social problems, with the exception of the overwhelming issue of enforced disappearances that we just mentioned.

This assumed bias has the merit of consistency and innovation, by juxtaposing studies on the right to food and on the right to safe drinking water by the corresponding mandate-holders, Olivier De Schutter and Catarina de Albuquerque, who make a balance of their work of six particularly outstanding years. We must also underline the essential diplomatic role of Ms. de Albuquerque in the negotiation of the Optional Protocol to the ICESCR. Two other mandates extend the work undertaken by the Sub-Commission on Human Rights, who had the merit of inscribing in the agenda of the Commission on Human Rights the issue of business and human rights. The lengthy road travelled for the adoption of the conceptual framework proposed by John Ruggie is analyzed in the study contributed by Michael K. Addo, Chair-Rapporteur of the Working Group on the issue of human rights and transnational corporations and other business enterprises. In addition, the Sub-Commission was also the starting point of the efforts undertaken for the adoption of the Guiding Principles on Extreme Poverty and Human Rights, which are the result of a special procedure that was spearheaded by Magdalena Sepúlveda. Another global challenge is highlighted by the new Special Rapporteur on human rights and the environment, through the study prepared by John H. Knox. How to go beyond mere procedural rights – such as access to information or the right to participation – and into the protection of substantive rights endangered by environmental harm? The issue of indigenous peoples' rights is also pertinent to this question.

We can see that the excellent contribution presented by our authors is an invitation to reflect upon these issues, and raises as many questions as it provides answers. One of the great merits of this collection is to have given voice to independent experts, who thus explain their "vision" of their mandate. At a time when certain groups want to limit the freedom of speech of independent experts through a code of conduct, these men and women from different continents combine a high ideal in accordance with the objectives and principles of the United Nations and a resolute determination to explore new approaches in an imaginative and pragmatic way. We must hope that other volumes edited in the same spirit will continue to present all the issues at the core of the work carried out by the United Nations. It is a very opportune timing to mark the 70th anniversary of the Charter of the United Nations, whose preamble strongly reaffirms the "*faith in fundamental human rights, in the dignity and worth of the human person, in the equal rights of men and women and of nations large and small.*"

CONTENTS

INTRODUCTION

Humberto Cantú Rivera[*]

This book is the result of a Professional Visiting Period I undertook at the Office of the High Commissioner for Human Rights in Geneva, in 2012. This period, during which I collaborated closely with the Sustainable Human Development Section of the Special Procedures Branch, included working in several of the tasks that are now reflected upon by the different contributors to the book. It allowed me to have access to the inner workings of the UN human rights machinery, and to better grasp the many challenges and areas of opportunities that – despite is gigantic work in such a tight budget – unfortunately still remain. But that is a topic for another discussion; there is no time to lose in the fight for the realization of human rights, and all the little and big efforts undertaken by the United Nations (and its frontline troops in the Special Procedures) in the field of human rights is a necessary one.

This book 'officially' starts (after the thoughtful foreword by Emmanuel Decaux) with a very special interview granted to me by Ms. Navi Pillay, the former UN High Commissioner for Human Rights, in early 2013. She reflects upon three different topics: freedom of expression and protection of journalists and human rights defenders in Latin America, sharing some examples of good practices in the region; the State duty to ensure access to effective remedies and reparation for victims of human rights violations, and the social effects of impunity and systematic infringements to human rights; and finally, on the role of NHRIs in preventing and sanctioning human rights abuses, and in providing integral assistance to victims. While short, Ms. Pillay provides a very clear insight as to the lines of action of her (now former) Office, and to some of the remaining challenges and good practices in the field of human rights.

* Associate Researcher for the Centre de recherche sur les droits de l'homme et le droit humanitaire (CRDH) of Université Panthéon-Assas (Paris II). Former Visiting Professional at the Office of the High Commissioner for Human Rights.

The first chapter deals with the history of human rights at the UN, and specifically with the early work of the Economic and Social Council and the Commission on Human Rights in setting up the latter's initial procedures. It then focuses on briefly describing the beginning of the Special Procedures, first in its country-based focus and its migration to thematic assessments and investigations, which set up the basis for the development of the system of Special Procedures as it's currently known, before addressing the politicization and demise of the Commission and the establishment of the Human Rights Council. The chapter turns to analyze the general characteristics and methods of work of the Special Procedures, to then address the flagship mechanism of the Council: the Universal Periodic Review. Several suggestions for improvement of the work of the Special Procedures and the Universal Periodic Review are shared throughout the chapter; however, it must be taken into consideration that the Universal Periodic Review is barely about to finish its second cycle, which will allow for a more complete assessment on its shortcomings and room for improvement.

The second chapter sees Olivier De Schutter, former UN Special Rapporteur on the right to food, provide his expert opinion on the status of the right to food in Latin America and the Caribbean. He divides his chapter in five subsections, where he treats many of the aspects he addressed during his mandate. The second subsection is devoted to the importance of the right to adequate food, where he briefly comments on its basic aspects and justification, and on the need to ensure effective access to this right for the most disadvantaged; a third subsection analyzes the status of the human right to food as a constitutional right throughout Latin America, and the contributions made by civil society and national human rights institutions for the establishment of this right at the constitutional level. Next, De Schutter focuses on the legal frameworks for the implementation of the right to food at the domestic level, addressing with a particular emphasis the development of nutrition and food security laws to complement the constitutional provisions establishing this right. In a fifth subsection, the former Special Rapporteur on the right to food analyzes the existing national strategies and public policies to ensure or contribute to the realization of this human right, highlighting the work of the UN Committee on Economic, Social and Cultural Rights regarding the need to adopt national strategies to ensure that nutrition and food security laws are effective. Finally, the sixth subsection concentrates on the analysis of several key elements of legal frameworks and public policies that may contribute to the realization of the right to adequate food, especially monitoring and accountability (through legal oversight, the role of national human rights institutions, regional and global monitoring, social movements, and the protection of human rights defenders) and effective implementation (via cross-sectoral coordination, participation, social programs' specificity, and budgetary allocations), before sharing some lessons learned in his experience on the right to food in Latin America.

The right to safe drinking water and sanitation is then addressed by Catarina de Albuquerque, former UN Special Rapporteur on the right to safe drinking water and sanitation, in the third chapter. Her contribution is particularly forward-looking, focusing on eliminating inequalities in sanitation, water and hygiene in the post-2015 agenda. She starts by analyzing non-discrimination, equality and equity as human rights principles that need to be included in the post-2015 agenda, to then turn to the elimination of inequalities as one of the missing pieces in the Millennium Development Goals. De Albuquerque argues that the inclusion of equality and non-discrimination as guiding human rights principles is paramount to the Sustainable Development Goals, which in her opinion should have a specific goal on ensuring equality. A final subsection in her chapter is devoted to the analysis of the goals that need to be reached to ensure equal access to safe drinking water, sanitation and hygiene: continue advancing while reducing inequalities; addressing geographical disparities, particularly between rural and urban zones and irregular settlements; generating hope in the most disadvantaged; facing the different group inequalities that exist in different countries; and addressing inequalities that depend on the individual characteristics of people, with a special focus on women and minorities. In concluding, she considers that the post-2015 agenda should explicitly include universal access to water, sanitation and hygiene, and that equality should be the underlying principle ensuring the right to water.

John H. Knox, the first UN Independent Expert and now first Special Rapporteur on human rights and the environment, shares his thoughts on moving the human rights and environment agenda forward. This article is of particular interest, given that at the time of writing, discussions were being held in Geneva over the possibility of extending his mandate for a further three years. His chapter thus focuses on the establishment of his mandate in 2012, on the relation between human rights and the environment, the historical context that led to the creation of the mandate, and on his first report to the Human Rights Council, in 2013. To achieve this, the second section of his chapter devotes some attention to two core issues: the link between environment and existing human rights, and the emergence of a human right to a healthy environment. A historical account detailing the many situations that led to the creation of the mandate appears next, relating how the Stockholm and Rio Declarations and the Ksentini Report, among others, weren't sufficient to eradicate the doubt surrounding the human rights and environment debate. However, the gradual inclusion by the Human Rights Council of resolutions related to climate change in 2008 eventually led to the creation of the mandate now led by John H. Knox. The final section of his chapter focuses on his preliminary report to the Human Rights Council, where he shares a list of the pending issues that at that moment in time needed to be analyzed by his mandate.

Michael K. Addo, Chair-Rapporteur of the UN Working Group on the issue of human rights and transnational corporations and other business enterprises, contributes the fifth chapter of the book, where he reflects upon the mandate entrusted to this Special Procedure. The issue of business and human rights has been a relevant topic for the better part of the last two decades, but hit a milestone in 2011 with the adoption by consensus of the UN Guiding Principles on Business and Human Rights. His chapter focuses on two main areas: the mandate entrusted to the Working Group by resolution A/HRC/RES/17/11, and the strategy adopted by its five members after its establishment in November 2011. His description of the tasks entrusted to the Working Group by the Human Rights Council is particularly objective: working closely with 193 countries and millions of transnational corporations, its subsidiaries and many other stakeholders is no easy feat. However, he remains optimistic to the idea of having a collaborative approach with all stakeholders involved. In relation to the strategy of the Working Group to implement his mandate, several key issues stand out: convergence in the integration and implementation of the Guiding Principles; the holistic and interrelated character of the 'Protect, Respect and Remedy Framework'; the issue of communications and access to effective remedies; the 'business case', and strategic partnerships. While this chapter was contributed barely after the first annual UN Forum on Business and Human Rights, it remains relevant in light of the extension of the mandate of the Working Group in September 2014. It can serve as a point of comparison between what he considered that should be the focus in the early days of the Working Group, and what they have been able to achieve in its first three years.

A sixth chapter, contributed by Olivier de Frouville, former Chair-Rapporteur of the UN Working Group on enforced or involuntary disappearances, relates to the twentieth anniversary of the UN Declaration for the Protection of All Persons from Enforced Disappearance, celebrated in 2012. It is particularly interesting how the English version of this text appears at a point in time where we just celebrated the 35th anniversary of the establishment of this UN Working Group, the first thematic procedure of the former Commission on Human Rights. A convenient coincidence, in my opinion. De Frouville briefly narrates the journey leading to the adoption of the UN Declaration in 1992, where references to the participation of Julio Cortázar in a conference in Paris on disappeared persons stand out because of their poetic resonance. He then concentrates in analyzing the role of the Working Group as interpreter and guardian of the Declaration, clearly identifying the different roles that are played by the Working Group and the Committee on Enforced Disappearances. He notes that for those countries that have not yet ratified the Convention, the Declaration continues to be a leading standard, and has the competence to receive individual communications from persons all over the world on the disappearance of their loved ones, whereas the Convention has an optional mechanism for the analysis of individual complaints. He closes his chapter by addressing some of the new challenges faced by the Working Group, particularly in light of the entry into force of the Convention and the establishment of the Committee.

Magdalena Sepúlveda Carmona, former UN Special Rapporteur on extreme poverty and human rights, shares an interesting chapter devoted to her experience in the mandate. She starts the chapter by sharing some brief notes on the Special Procedures of the Human Rights Council, to then turn to the financial context during the time when she was appointed as mandate-holder. She recalls that this led to her decision to partially focus her mandate on social protection programs, as a means to provide poverty relief to people. Similarly to Catarina de Albuquerque, she considers that the principles of equality and non-discrimination, participation, transparency and accountability need to be included in the whole process of development and implementation of social protection programs. Thus, the second section of her chapter is devoted entirely to analyze the characteristics and principles of a human rights-based approach in the context of social protection. The final section of her chapter is devoted to analyzing the Guiding Principles on extreme poverty and human rights, adopted by the Human Rights Council in September 2012. The rationale behind them lies in ensuring that public policies reach the poorest and most disadvantaged, and to give them a voice in the discussion of public policies affecting them.

The contribution of Catalina Rivera Díaz, First General Attorney on Human Rights for the Human Rights Commission of Nuevo Leon (Mexico), focuses on victims, communications and the Special Procedures of the Human Rights Council. This seventh chapter starts by making a historic narrative of the development of the communications procedure in the work of the Commission on Human Rights since its early days, which were definitely established with the creation of the Working Group on enforced or involuntary disappearances. Ms. Rivera then analyzes the development of a more or less standardized communications procedure by the early thematic mandates of the Commission on Human Rights, to then turn to a quantitative analysis based on the latest communications report issued by Special Procedures mandate-holders. As it turns out from her analysis, it appears that the system of individual communications to mandate-holders has had a middling efficacy; however, it is particularly helpful to identify, even in our day and age where human rights are virtually everywhere, the 'top ten' human rights issues around the world. Surprisingly, only one of the economic, social and cultural rights appears in that list. She closes her chapter by analyzing the purported role of communications as a quasi-jurisdictional procedure, before turning to an analysis of the characteristics and 'benefits' of this system.

The final chapter in this edited volume belongs to Minerva Martínez Garza, President of the Human Rights Commission of Nuevo Leon. Her contribution focuses on the interaction of national human rights institutions with the UN human rights machinery. She starts her chapter by revisiting the Paris Principles of 1993, from which she identifies four core functions of NHRIs: analysis, harmonization, international cooperation, and awareness-raising. She then devotes the next section to analyze the interaction between international human rights law and domestic law, and the particularly prominent role that NHRIs can play in promoting the use and ensuring the effectiveness of international law at the national level. The final section of her chapter revolves around increasing the role played by NHRIs at the domestic level, with a specific focus on Mexico, where she makes clear that their work in monitoring the Government and other non-State actors is one of the keys to ensuring the effectiveness of international human rights law.

The different chapters included in this volume attest to the diversity of challenges and achievements made by the Special Procedures of the Human Rights Council. While Special Procedures mandate-holders have recently been under intense scrutiny, particularly from some Governments with dubious human rights records, their work in advancing human rights protection through monitoring and individual communications, standard setting and country visits remains the best that international human rights law can currently offer. Their coherent, coordinated work and the diversity of topics they cover has greatly contributed to the development of soft standards in this field, improving the protection of human rights and reaffirming the interrelated character of civil, political, economic, social and cultural rights.

On this note, I wish to close by once more expressing my sincere gratitude to all the contributors to this edited volume. It is to be understood that all of these contributions were made in the contributors' personal capacities, and do not necessarily reflect the views of the United Nations, the Office of the High Commissioner for Human Rights, the Human Rights Council or the mandates that they represent, nor of the Human Rights Commission of Nuevo Leon. This volume is the English version of *El futuro es hoy: construyendo una agenda de derechos humanos*, published in Spanish by the Human Rights Commission of Nuevo Leon and Universidad Autonoma de Nuevo Leon in 2014. While several of the manuscripts were originally delivered in English, some translation and editing work was undertaken by the editor of this volume. Of course, any mistakes remain solely my own.

Paris, France
15 March 2015

INTERVIEW WITH NAVI PILLAY, FORMER UN HIGH COMMISSIONER FOR HUMAN RIGHTS*

Navanethem (Navi) Pillay is the former UN High Commissioner for Human Rights. A South-African national, she started her tenure as head of the Office of the High Commissioner for Human Rights on 1 September 2008, after the United Nations General Assembly approved her appointment in July of that same year. With an original mandate of four years, it was extended for a further two years starting on 1 September 2012. After six years as High Commissioner, she finished her appointment on 31 August 2014.

Prior to her appointment as High Commissioner, Navi Pillay already had an important legal career at the international level. Between 1995 and 2003, she was a judge on the International Criminal Tribunal for Rwanda, where she served the last four years as President. Between 2003 and August 2008 she was a judge on the International Criminal Court, the first permanent international criminal tribunal.

In South Africa, she acted as a defense attorney for anti-apartheid activists, and in 1995 she was appointed as acting judge on the South African High Court. She received a BA and a LLB from Natal University in South Africa, as well as a Master of Laws and a Doctorate of Juridical Science from Harvard University.

In October 2012, the Human Rights Commission of Nuevo Leon (Mexico) requested the High Commissioner for Human Rights to grant an exclusive interview, looking to obtain her opinion and thoughts on topics of importance to Mexico and Latin America in general. The interview revolved around three particular topics. The first one was in relation to one of the

* This interview was granted to Humberto Cantú Rivera in early 2013, who was a Visiting Professional during the second semester of 2012 in the Special Procedures Branch of the Office of the High Commissioner for Human Rights. As of that moment, the UN High Commissioner for Human Rights was Navi Pillay. Since September 2014, the current High Commissioner is Zeid Ra'ad Al Hussein.

most important and relevant topics for Mexico, regarding the protection of journalists and human rights defenders, as well as freedom of expression.

A second issue that was discussed during the interview was the obligation of the State to provide access to effective and opportune remedies, and on the right of victims of human rights violations to reparation. In addition, the question of the social effects of impunity and systematic violations of human rights was canvassed.

Finally, the High Commissioner for Human Rights shared some of her impressions regarding the role of national human rights institutions (NHRIs) in the prevention and sanction of abuses by the State or its agents, as well as regarding the integral assistance that must be provided by NHRIs to victims of human rights violations.

The following paragraphs transcribe verbatim the interview to Navi Pillay.

Q1: What do you think of the current state of freedom of expression and the protection of journalists and human rights defenders in Latin America? What kind of national systems should be put in place for their protection, in your experience? Any positive examples?

The situation of human rights defenders is a cause for concern in several countries in Latin America. Human rights defenders are frequently subjected to threats, attacks and intimidation by a variety of actors, very often from non-state actors. Many human rights defenders also face accusations and even legal proceedings because of their role in defending human rights. This amounts to criminalizing their work.

Journalists, who also play an important role in the defense of freedom of expression and human rights, have been the target of similar attacks. One important step towards improving the protection of human rights defenders is for governments to publicly recognize their vital contribution to democracy, justice and the rule of law. And equally important, those who violate their human rights must be held accountable. Attacks should be adequately investigated, and those responsible brought to justice without delay and with the full force of the law.

There are several positive examples of systems for the protection of human rights defenders, even if further improvements could still be made.

Colombia, for example, has developed some effective mechanisms for the protection of human rights defenders. And in Mexico, the adoption of the Law for the Protection of Human Rights Defenders and Journalists (*Ley para la Protección de Personas Defensoras de Derechos Humanos y Periodistas)* offers an opportunity to address this critical issue. My office in Mexico has been working closely with the Mexican authorities on this law, and the crucial issue of how it is implemented. The mechanisms developed and lessons learned in Colombia can also contribute to the development of effective mechanisms in Mexico.

Q2: States have an obligation to ensure remedy and reparation for victims of human rights violations – can you elaborate on this obligation? What are the different approaches in this regard?

States have a wide range of obligations towards the victims of human rights violations. These rights have been established in a number of international instruments, such as the "Basic Principles and Guidelines on the Right to a Remedy and Reparation for Victims of Gross Violations of International Human Rights Law and Serious Violations of International Humanitarian Law" (the so-called Remedy Principles), which were adopted by the United Nations General Assembly on 16 December 2005.

Victims' rights include the right of access to justice, to reparations for the harm suffered, and of access to information concerning the violations committed, as well as relevant remedies. When the human rights violations committed are attributable to the State, the State should provide adequate, effective and prompt reparations to the victims. In the event that other parties are liable for the harm suffered, States should endeavour to establish national reparations programmes when these parties are unable or unwilling to meet their obligations.

Reparation programmes seek to redress systemic violations of human rights by providing a range of material and symbolic benefits to victims. Reparations can include direct support such as monetary compensation, medical and psychological services, health care, educational support, return of property or compensation for its loss. They may also include important overarching acts such as official public apologies, the construction of museums and memorials, and establishment of days of commemoration. Reparations programmes can also form quick, visible and effective complements to truth-seeking processes and prosecution initiatives, by providing concrete remedies to victims, promoting reconciliation, and restoring public trust in the State.

What are the social effects of impunity and systematic violations of human rights?

Impunity arises from a failure by States to meet their obligations to investigate, prosecute, try and sanction those responsible for human rights violations; a failure to provide victims with effective remedies and to ensure that they receive reparations for the injuries suffered; and a failure to satisfy their right to know the truth about violations. Ending impunity is the best guarantee to prevent a recurrence of violations, as it sends a powerful message that they will not be tolerated. On the contrary, allowing impunity to prevail simply perpetuates crime and encourages further violations against the population. It emboldens those who commit such crimes, thus corroding the rule of law and undermining the democratic fabric of the nation.

Q3: What should be the fundamental role of national human rights institutions in the prevention and sanction of abuses carried out by the State or its agents, as well as in providing integral assistance to victims?

The Principles relating to the status of national institutions adopted by the UN General Assembly in 1993 – also called the Paris Principles – establish internationally accepted standards on the role and functions of National Human Rights Institutions (NHRIs). According to these Principles, monitoring is a key element of NHRIs' mandate. NHRIs can monitor domestic human rights situations, government policy and action, make inquiries into human rights issues and violations, and handle individual complaints. No public entity should be excluded from the monitoring function of NHRIs. In particular, law enforcement agencies such as the police, the army, intelligence services and other security services, should be subject to NHRI scrutiny.

NHRIs should also have the power to visit all places of detention, including those run by the police, the army and the intelligence services. NHRIs' regular visits to such places of detention, with minimal notice, contribute to the prevention of human rights violations, especially torture and other forms of cruel or inhumane treatment, as well as violations of due process guarantees.

NHRIs mandated to receive complaints should have broad powers to deal with them. No relevant public body should be excluded from their jurisdiction. Consequently, victims of human rights violations by the State or its agents should be able to file complaints to the NHRI. The NHRI shall investigate all complaints received, assess and analyse them, collect information and evidence as required, refer cases to the judicial system and cooperate with the concerned authorities in finding remedial solutions for these cases. The NHRI shall indicate to the victims all remedies available to them and promote victims' access to these remedies.

The Paris Principles state that NHRIs should make recommendations to the competent authorities and should propose amendments to laws, regulations and administrative practices, especially if they lie at the root of the difficulties encountered by the people filing the petitions in order to assert their rights. NHRIs should also monitor government departments' compliance with their advice and recommendations.

THE UNITED NATIONS HUMAN RIGHTS COUNCIL

Remarks on Its History, Procedures, Challenges and Perspectives

Humberto CANTÚ RIVERA*

I. INTRODUCTION

Human rights have been at the core of the United Nations since its foundation. They have been one of the banners and interests promoted and protected at the international level by the organization, in addition to peace, security and development. It was necessary to establish an international organization to deal specifically and exclusively with issues related to human prerogatives, in order to set a direction and lead the international opinion on the topic.

However, after several decades of work, the reality was different than what had been foreseen at the beginning of this political project. This led to a need for change, to restructure and amend the situations that undermined the efficacy of the organs in charge of protecting human rights. Therefore, a transition from a Commission on Human Rights to a new Human Rights Council took place, in an effort to reestablish the trust of the Member States to the United Nations in the bodies, mechanisms and structures whose mandate dealt with the protection of human rights.

This reform concluded (or perhaps started) in 2006, presenting the Human Rights Council with the opportunity to start its own rebuilding. Thus, given the mandate of the General Assembly, the Special Procedures existing under the Commission were streamlined, the complaints mechanism was reformed, the internal organs of the Commission were transformed, and a

* Associate Researcher for the Centre de recherche sur les droits de l'homme et le droit humanitaire (CRDH) of Université Panthéon-Assas (Paris II). Former Visiting Professional at the Office of the High Commissioner for Human Rights.

new stalwart mechanism that pretends to be a platform allowing States to self-assess their performance and compliance in the field of human rights, and to receive feedback from its peers was created. The latter was an effort to have a universal and non-politicized procedure that would overcome the ideological barriers that led to the Commission's reform.

This chapter seeks to briefly discuss the history of the Commission on Human Rights, and the conditions that led to its replacement. In addition, it will look into the structure, functions, problems and virtues of the Special Procedures. Finally, it will briefly analyze the functions and early reactions to the Universal Periodic Review, which has recently finished its second cycle.

II. THE HISTORICAL SIDE: FROM THE COMMISSION ON HUMAN RIGHTS TO THE HUMAN RIGHTS COUNCIL

The Commission on Human Rights was one of the bodies contemplated in the initial structure of the United Nations. Article 68 of the UN Charter gave birth to the Commission, by determining that the Economic and Social Council (ECOSOC) would establish commissions "in economic and social fields and for the promotion of human rights..."[1] Thus, the protection of human rights was consolidated in 1945 as one of the lines of action of the organization, through the work that would be undertaken by the Commission on Human Rights.

Through resolution 5(I)[2] of 16 February 1946, the Economic and Social Council determined to establish a Commission on Human Rights, in accordance with the mandate of article 68 of the Charter. The second paragraph of the resolution set forth that the work of the Commission would consist in submitting proposals, recommendations and reports regarding the drafting of an international bill of rights, of international declarations or conventions on civil liberties, on the status of women, on

1 *Charter of the United Nations* (26 June 1945), Article 68.

2 Based on the *Report of the Committee on the Organization of the Economic and Social Council*, UN Doc. E/20 (15 February 1946), through which a drafting Sub-Committee informed the Committee on the establishment of several subsidiary organs to the ECOSOC, among them the Commission on Human Rights.

freedom of information, on the protection of minorities and the prevention of discrimination.[3] It was also determined that the Commission would have nine initial members.[4]

After the establishment of the nuclear Commission, the preparatory work for the determination of the terms of reference of the Commission on Human Rights took place.[5] On 21 June 1946, the Economic and Social Council of the UN adopted resolution E/RES/9(II), where it addressed different aspects that were deemed necessary to fulfill the mandate set forth in the Charter. Thus, taking into consideration the report of the nuclear Commission, resolution E/RES/9(II) took up the functions established by the ECOSOC in the second paragraph of resolution 5(I), while adding a *sub-paragraph e* that included the provision that the Commission on Human Rights would have competence over any type of issue related to human rights that was not already contemplated in the four preceding paragraphs (international bill of human rights, international human rights instruments, protection of minorities and prevention of discrimination). In relation to its composition, it was determined that the Commission would initially have one representative of each of the 18 Member States to the United Nations, who would be nominated by their country and ratified by the Economic and Social Council for a three-year mandate.

The Commission would also have the possibility of calling *ad hoc* experts, configured either in working groups or individually, which would eventually become the Special Procedures. That resolution determined that pending the adoption of an international bill of human rights, international treaties involving basic human rights (including peace treaties) would serve as fundamental standards for the protection of human prerogatives.

3 Doc. E/20 (15 February 1946), p. 3.

4 The Representatives of Norway (Paal Berg), France (René Cassin), Belgium (Fernand Dehousse), Peru (Víctor Paul Haya de la Torre), India (K. C. Neogi), United States of America (Eleanor Roosevelt), China (John C. H. Wu), the USSR (Alexander Borisov) and Yugoslavia (Dusan Brkish).

5 Commission on Human Rights, *Report of the Commission on Human Rights to the Second Session of the Economic and Social Council*, Doc. E/38/Rev.1 (21 May 1946). The content of this document was taken from the *Draft Resolution Concerning the Report of the Commission on Human Rights*, UN Doc. E/56/Rev.1 (19 June 1946) presented by the Drafting Committee on the Social Commissions, which would become the basis of the resolution that finally determined the competence and permanent organization of the Commission.

Lastly, the resolution determined the creation of three Sub-Commissions that would contribute to the work of the Commission: a Sub-Commission on Freedom of Information and of the Press,[6] a Sub-Commission on the Protection of Minorities,[7] and a Sub-Commission on the Prevention of Discrimination.[8]

In its first session between 27 January and 10 February 1947, the Commission established a group to work on the draft international bill of human rights, as well as the Sub-Commissions on freedom of information and of the press, on the protection of minorities and on the prevention of discrimination.[9] It was also determined then that the Commission would receive communications concerning human rights,[10] despite paragraph 22 of that same document stating that the Commission didn't have powers to act on the complaints, which would nevertheless be contrary to the provision of sub-paragraph e of resolution E/RES/9(II). This provision would undoubtedly become the basis for the functioning of human rights treaty bodies, which can receive complaints and monitor implementation of the corresponding treaties, or of the communications that may be presented to the current Human Rights Council or to the different Special Procedures mandates.[11]

---

6 The mandate of the Sub-Commission would consist on determining the rights, obligations and practices that conformed the concept of freedom of information.

7 Its mandate was to examine the provisions that should be adopted for the definition of the principles applicable to the protection of minorities, and to make recommendations to the Commission.

8 Its function was to examine the provisions that should be adopted to define the principles related to the prevention of discrimination, and to make recommendations to the Committee thereon.

9 Commission on Human Rights, *Report to the Economic and Social Council on the First Session of the Commission*, Doc. E/259 (1947).

10 *Id.*, par. 21; for a more detailed analysis of the communications sent to Special Procedures, see Catalina Rivera Diaz' chapter in this book.

11 Later on, resolution 1503 (XLVIII) of 27 May 1970 established a confidential procedure – known as *Procedure 1503* – through which the Sub-Commission for the Prevention of Discrimination and the Protection of Minorities would call a group of experts to review the complaints and communications alleging the existence of patterns of grave human rights violations, and in case the allegations were confirmed, to report it to the Sub-Commission. This procedure existed as such until its amendment in 2000, prior to its substitution by a new complaints mechanism after the Human Rights Council was installed through resolution 5/1 of 18 June 2007. However, this complaints mechanism is different than the one instituted under the mandates of the working groups, independent experts and special rapporteurs; we will address this in the following section.

The facts following these developments are well-known: the adoption of the Universal Declaration of Human Rights in 1948, followed by the International Covenant on Economic, Social and Cultural Rights and the International Covenant on Civil and Political Rights in 1966 led to the consolidation of the International Bill of Human Rights. The Commission gradually went from 18 to 53 members[12] from all the geographic regions of the world, and seven international conventions related to the protection of human rights were adopted.[13]

The Special Procedures started in 1967, when international pressure forced the Commission to establish an *ad hoc* study group to investigate the human rights situation in South Africa.[14] Ten years later, it established a second *ad hoc* working group to investigate the human rights situation in Chile, in what would be the first country mandates. In 1979, the Commission on Human Rights determined to replace the working group in Chile with one special rapporteur and two experts, in order to study the fate of the disappeared during the Pinochet dictatorship, giving birth to the first thematic special procedure of the Commission: the Working Group on Enforced of Involuntary Disappearances.[15] This group of independent experts started its mandate in 1980 and still operates to this day, as the guardian of the UN Declaration on the Protection of All Persons

---

12 The 18 Member States in 1946 increased to 21 in 1962, to 32 in 1967, to 43 in 1979 and finally to 53 Member States in 1992.

13 The Convention on the Rights of Persons with Disabilities (13 December 2006) and the International Convention for the Protection of all Persons from Enforced Disappearance (20 December 2006) were adopted when the Human Rights Council had already begun its work, after substituting the Commission on Human Rights.

14 Economic and Social Council, Res. 1235 (XLII), (6 June 1967). In this resolution, the ECOSOC authorized the Commission and the Sub-Commission to examine the relevant information and to undertake the necessary studies regarding the grave human rights and fundamental freedoms violations in South Africa resulting *inter alia* from the policy of apartheid. Said resolution was the basis for the establishment of the future thematic and country special procedures, regardless of the *sui generis* nature of the mechanism as set forth in the resolution. See J. GUTTER, 'Special Procedures and the Human Rights Council: Achievements and Challenges Ahead' (2007) 7:1 *HRLR (Human Rights Law Review)* 93, 97.

15 The establishment of the UN Working Group on Enforced or Involuntary Disappearances was the beginning of the era of thematic procedures. This approach allowed the Commission on Human Rights to have a less controversial method to monitor the main global human rights issues, resulting in a politically viable option to work with. *Id.*, pp. 98–99.

from Enforced Disappearance.[16] In 1990, the Special Procedures of the Commission on Human Rights had already extended to cover six specific issues: enforced disappearances; extrajudicial, summary or arbitrary executions; religious intolerance; mercenaries; torture, and the sale of children. Since then, many other topics have been analyzed by the different experts and working groups, covering the whole human rights spectrum.

However, one of the main obstacles the Commission on Human Rights faced was the gradual loss of credibility before the international society as a result of its "politicization",[17] which can be more aptly related to the practice of regional bloc politics. It was clear that many of the 53 members to the Commission on Human Rights sought access to avoid having their human rights record monitored, or in order to criticize the performance of other States.[18] This situation, in addition to debates that yielded little to no success in relation to the protection and promotion of human rights, led the Secretary-General of the United Nations to propose its substitution by a smaller, less politicized body, the Human Rights Council.[19]

---

16 Please refer to the article prepared for this edited volume by Olivier de Frouville, former Chair-Rapporteur of the UN Working Group on Enforced or Involuntary Disappearance, for a specific insight on the role of the Working Group.

17 Which however was a natural expectation on the line of work of the Commission, given its intergovernmental nature. Nevertheless, the General Assembly stated this in resolution 60/251, by mentioning that in spite of the recognition to the history and achievements of the Commission, it was necessary to ensure its universality and objectivity, and to eliminate the selective character that existed regarding certain human rights issues, the application of double standards and its politicization.

18 Alston notes, for example, that there were certain political issues that some countries sought to leave outside the reach of the Commission on Human Rights, while some of them sought to avoid the creation of a general and universal monitoring system. See P. ALSTON, 'The Commission on Human Rights' in P. ALSTON (ed.), *The United Nations and Human Rights: A Critical Appraisal*, Oxford University Press, Oxford 1992, p. 142.

19 For some, the reform of the human rights machinery was the result of the political impossibility to transform the rest of the United Nations' bodies, in particular the Security Council and the General Assembly. Thus, the reform and substitution of the Commission on Human Rights sought to present an image of consensus and reform, despite the changes only affected the human rights machinery. See O. DE FROUVILLE, 'Building a Universal System for the Protection of Human Rights: The Way Forward' in M.C. BASSIOUNI and W.A. SCHABAS (eds.), *New Challenges for the UN Human Rights Machinery. What Future for the UN Treaty Body System and the Human Rights Council Procedures?*, Intersentia, Cambridge 2011, p. 242.

The General Assembly adopted resolution A/RES/60/251 on 3 April 2006, recognizing the contributions made by the Commission on Human Rights to the development of this branch of international law, and determining in its first paragraph to substitute the Commission by a Human Rights Council, which would be a subsidiary organ to the General Assembly. The Human Rights Council would be composed of 47 Member States, elected by secret ballot by the majority of the members of the General Assembly, and subject to the newly created Universal Periodic Review. In addition, the General Assembly determined that the Member States would have as a duty the promotion of the respect of human rights, and the commitment to uphold the highest standards to that end.

The substitution of the Commission by the Human Rights Council was generally well received, for it presented an opportunity to start working from scratch in the field of human rights. It also allowed the Council to address those situations and contexts that had led to the loss of credibility of the former Commission. The establishment of new mechanisms and the substitution of the structure of the subsidiary organs of the Commission, however, brought different challenges, which also served to adopt several reforms that allowed to have a more strict control over the work in the human rights field, a situation that we will address in the following sections.

III. THE SPECIAL PROCEDURES

The creation of the Human Rights Council presented the opportunity to renew its structures, mechanisms and procedures, and generated an international sense of optimism.[20] The fact that the reform was determined in New York by the General Assembly through resolution 60/251, but that its analysis and instrumentation were decided in Geneva through resolution 5/1 of the Council,[21] allowed for a constructive and realistic debate on the needs of the new organ.

---

20 Upton considers that the creation of a new human rights organ within the United Nations reflected the acceptance by States of the importance to improve the global promotion and protection of human rights. See H. UPTON, 'The Human Rights Council: First Impressions and Future Challenges' (2007) 7:1 *HRLR* 29, 39.

21 Human Rights Council, *Institution-building of the United Nations Human Rights Council*, A/HRC/RES/5/1 (18 June 2007).

Different processes started: first, it was determined that it would be necessary to rationalize the special procedures, in order to avoid duplicity in the performance of the work undertaken, as well as to establish codes of conduct for the mandate-holders, regardless of their capacity as Independent Experts, Special Rapporteurs, Special Representatives or Working Groups.[22] It was also determined to substitute the Sub-Commission for the Promotion and Protection of Human Rights – which had so far been a relatively autonomous organ with the liberty to conduct its own investigations and projects, establish mandates and review communications filed through the complaints procedure – for an Advisory Committee, a subsidiary organ to the Council conformed by 18 experts that would act under its orders and control. However, its attributions were limited in relation to those of the Sub-Commission, given that resolution 5/1 of the Human Rights Council determined that the Advisory Committee would not be able to adopt resolutions, and its investigative contributions would be at the request of the Council.

The establishment of the Universal Periodic Review was another of the new attributions granted to the successor of the Commission on Human Rights, which sought to create a mechanism that would directly address (at least theoretically) the politicization that surrounded the Commission.[23] Thus, this

22 A debate exists regarding the need to clarify the terminology used in the appointment of mandate-holders. Thus, it has been proposed that the appointment as Special Rapporteur is given only to those mandates that have as their objective the monitoring and protection of human rights, in addition to the development of a specific issue of this branch of international law. On the contrary, the appointment as Independent Expert or Special Representative shall be used only for those mandates that have as their objective the study of specific issues and questions in the human rights field. See I. NIFOSI-SUTTON, 'The System of the UN Special Procedures: Some Proposals for Change' in M.C. BASSIOUNI and W.A. SCHABAS (eds.), *New Challenges for the UN Human Rights Machinery. What Future for the UN Treaty Body System and the Human Rights Council Procedures?*, Intersentia, Cambridge 2011, pp. 408–409.

23 Ripert mentions that the problem becomes more difficult because the debate on human rights inevitably overlaps with the debate on the United Nations and the universality of an administrative system for the international community. Therefore, the result is the adoption of positions according to the interests of States, which invariably has a political connotation. This constitutes a polarization between particularism and universalism, as well as between the different groups that come together to support the causes that derive from national and regional interests. See J.M. RIPERT, 'Les organes principaux de l'ONU: Les droits de l'homme entre New York et Genève' in E. DECAUX (dir.), *Les Nations Unies et les*

new mechanism would ensure that the Human Rights Council would analyze the human rights record of all UN Member States. Conversely, the former Procedure 1503 would be modified, in order to address the gaps that had been for a long time pointed out by different stakeholders. All these measures were adopted with the aim of making the Human Rights Council a more efficient, transparent and pragmatic intergovernmental body that would work more effectively in the promotion and protection of human rights.

One of the main achievements of the transition between the Commission and the Council was the continuity of the special procedures.[24] The special procedures are a series of mandates entrusted to experts who work independently from any State or organization, and whose general purpose is the development of specific issues of international human rights law, to monitor the application and respect of human rights in States, and in many cases to receive communications regarding alleged human rights violations that may work as quasi-jurisdictional procedures at the international level. Even if the different mandates are independent from each other, many of them are interconnected and work in a collaborative manner,[25] constituting a system of special procedures for the protection and promotion of human rights.[26]

In December 2014, the Special Procedures of the Human Rights Council have 39 thematic mandates related to a broad range of issues related to human rights, covering the spheres of civil, political, economic, social, cultural and environmental rights. They are one of the most positive and productive initiatives that are part of the legacy of the Commission on

---

droits de l'homme, Pedone, Paris 2006, p. 68. The Universal Periodic Review thus presented itself as an opportunity to overcome that political struggle.

24 See C. CALLEJÓN, 'Developments at the Human Rights Council in 2007: A Reflection of its Ambivalence', (2008) 8:2 *HRLR* 323, 324–325.

25 That is the case, for example, of the mandates related to the rights to adequate housing, to health, to water or to food, all deriving from articles 11 and 12 of the International Covenant on Economic, Social and Cultural Rights.

26 Despite not being initially considered as such, since 1993 the special procedures became a system, developing structures that allow them to act in a coordinated manner. Gutter considers that as a system, special procedures have three impacts: a consolidated institutional progress; the institutionalization of a comprehensive UN focus on human rights; and practical consequences (such as the establishment of standardized methods of work) as a result of the annual meetings of mandate-holders and the work of the Coordination Committee of Special Procedures. See J. GUTTER, above n 14, at 100; and I. NIFOSI-SUTTON, above n 22, at 402.

Human Rights, which managed to survive certain attacks and reticence with respect to their conservation as a procedure during the last years of the Commission.[27] The thematic mandates have as a general purpose the analysis of relevant issues for the realization of the human right whose protection has been entrusted.

Pedagogically, thematic mandates can be divided in two groups: the first one includes those mandates dealing with specific questions and rights, tending to the adoption of actions for the effective protection of human rights (as those rights related to the personal freedoms and fundamental human rights, such as freedom of expression, human rights defenders or arbitrary detentions). The second group includes those mandates concentrated on questions related to ascertainable rights, where the activities are directed to the clarification and determination of a particular human right, and thus to its interpretation, correct application and respect (such as the human rights to safe-drinking water, to food or to a healthy environment, or the implications and effect of extreme poverty on human rights, for example).

Among the general functions of thematic mandates are, for example, the analysis of specific phenomena and their impact on human rights, the exploration of challenges and trends regarding the protection of vulnerable groups, the clarification of the normative content of rights, consultations with other experts or stakeholders (in order to have a global and more specific perspective on the different difficulties for the effective protection of human rights), or the drafting of non-binding instruments and the contributions needed for their implementation. Of course, those functions vary in accordance with the mandate, depending of the type of challenges or issues that a specific mandate may face.

Moreover, there are currently 14 country mandates, of which 13 are active (Belarus, Cambodia, Central African Republic, Côte d'Ivoire, Eritrea, North Korea, Haiti, Iran, Mali, Myanmar, the Palestinian territories, Somalia and Sudan) and one shall start in the near future (Syria, which

---

[27] As a result of the rejection against them, the policy of rationalization of special procedures was adopted, in an effort by certain countries to restrict their powers and functions. For a broader perspective on this, see P.S. PINHEIRO, 'Les Etats au sein de la Commission des droits de l'homme, la politisation des groupes' in E. DECAUX (dir.), *Les Nations Unies et les droits de l'homme*, Pedone, Paris 2006, p. 107; and J. GUTTER, above n 14, at 105.

will start once the mandate of the commission of inquiry ends). These mandates, contrary to the attributions and basis of thematic mandates, have as their purpose the analysis of situations that may constitute human rights violations within the territory of certain States.

The special procedures generally have a mechanism that is shared by both thematic and country mandates: on site-visits. Through these, mandate-holders visit the States they deem pertinent (or in the case of country mandates, the country that is to be analyzed by the mandate), with the objective of obtaining information from primary sources regarding the human rights situations, as well as to assess the situation and propose appropriate measures and recommendations to ensure a better protection and respect of international standards. In the case of thematic mandates, the experts or working groups also have the possibility of undertaking follow-up visits, to verify the extent to which their recommendations were applied.[28]

In addition, some thematic mandates have the competence to receive communications on alleged violations or situations affecting the right that the mandate covers, with the aim of being a quasi-jurisdictional procedure at the international level. This allows the parties (the affected individual, group or organization and the State) to try to resolve the issue through mediation, in full respect of the human rights of the real or potential victims and in compliance with the international obligations of the State.[29] There are two types of communications, depending on the seriousness and urgency: *allegation letters* and *urgent appeals*.

Allegation letters are communications used when a human rights violation has taken place. They are intended to make the Special Rapporteur, Independent Expert or Working Group draw the attention

---

28 On this, see I. NIFOSI-SUTTON, above n 22, at 394.

29 See M. KOTHARI, 'From Commission to the Council: Evolution of UN Charter Bodies' in D. SHELTON (ed.), *The Oxford Handbook of International Human Rights Law*, Oxford University Press, Oxford 2013, p. 605: "Unlike the complaint mechanisms of treaty bodies or the Council's 1503 procedure, SPs can receive information from sources that have not exhausted domestic remedies, making them a powerful avenue for victims, or their defenders, to reach an international mechanism and contribute to pressure being placed on governments to halt violations and to overhaul weak and cumbersome national mechanisms for access to justice. [This] arguably means that adjudication and a quasi-judicial function for SPs is becoming accepted standard practice at the Council."

of the corresponding Government on the issue, in order for it to take the appropriate measures to investigate and resolve the allegations against it, and to communicate the measures adopted and the results of the investigation. On the contrary, *urgent appeals* are used in those cases in which the human rights violation has not been committed but is likely to occur, having as its purpose that the corresponding Government prevents it. Generally, urgent appeals will only be used in cases of grave human rights violations, if the personal integrity or the life of an individual or group is in danger, or if the question is of such a nature that it cannot be addressed adequately through an allegation letter.

Even if these communications procedures are not meant to be adversarial or even remotely judicial – their nature is entirely preventive –, Governments have the opportunity to present the requested information within a reasonable period of time, in order for the UN expert to determine whether it is pertinent to make recommendations to the State or not. A report on the communications issued by the mandates (which can be joint if two or more human rights are affected) is presented before every regular session of the Human Rights Council, where the responses and measures adopted by Governments as well as the statistics relating to the communications filed against them are included.[30]

These tools have been the basis for the stability of the special procedures system and for the confrontation that existed in the last years of the Commission on Human Rights. Nevertheless, in spite of the relative success they've had in the development of regulatory standards in a broad range of human rights, the special procedures face several difficulties to provide a more effective protection.[31] Leaving aside financial and human resources

---

30 Despite being brought before the Human Rights Council, communications and reports about them don't receive the necessary attention from States, which obviously renders any improvement in human rights protection more difficult. See T. BALDWIN-PASK and P. SCANNELLA, 'The Unfinished Business of a Special Procedures System' in M.C. BASSIOUNI and W.A. SCHABAS (eds.), *New Challenges for the UN Human Rights Machinery. What Future for the UN Treaty Body System and the Human Rights Council Procedures?*, Intersentia, Cambridge 2011, p. 445.

31 Callejón considers that generally the reconstruction of the Council reflected the ambivalence of the reform, by having to strengthen the special procedures system on one side, and accomplish its rationalization on the other. For a more precise insight, see C. CALLEJÓN, above n 24, at 324; and for a general overview on the

issues, which undoubtedly are important limitations for the appropriate functioning of the special procedures (and in particular for the support provided by staff at the Office of the High Commissioner for Human Rights), the following paragraphs will focus on describing some of the main problems that UN experts face in this field.

One of the eternal problems that human rights have faced is on obtaining a genuine cooperation from States. This cooperation is irremediably necessary if an improvement in the standards of living of individuals and groups, and thus a better protection of their rights, is to be expected. This cooperation must exist not only in the form of financial contributions made by States for the functioning and permanence of the system, but also in relation to the substantive content over which special procedures work. Without an adequate implementation of the reforms made by mandate-holders, without the appropriate follow-up to the communications received, and without an active, engaged and genuine participation to achieve a real development in the protection of human rights, these will continue to be at the mercy of the political will and interests of States.[32]

From a different standpoint, one of the difficulties being faced by the special procedures system lies in the limitations imposed by the actions of the Human Rights Council, particularly in relation to time. If the establishment of a permanent body (the Council) in substitution of a six-week annual gathering (of the former Commission) could mean an improvement in dealing with all the issues related to the protection of human rights, the reality shows that the sessions of the Human Rights Council do not suffice to give proper consideration to the reports presented by the Special Rapporteurs, Independent Experts or Working Groups.

In addition to the insufficient economic and human resources available, the aforementioned is also a limitation to perform the necessary follow-up to

---

substitution of the Commission by the Council, see C. CALLEJÓN, *La réforme de la Commission des droits de l'homme des Nations Unies: de la Commission au Conseil*, Pedone, Paris 2008.

32 As mentioned by Hampson, due to the lack of a police or regulatory body, an international judicial or quasi-judicial system needs the support of a political body if their pronouncements are to have any real effect. See F.J. HAMPSON, 'An Overview of the Reform of the UN Human Rights Machinery' (2007) 7:1 *HRLR* 7, 12.

the implementation of recommendations made by experts, given that their participation and that of States, NHRIs, other intergovernmental bodies, and NGOs prevent or render difficult an organization and administration that is sufficient to tend to all the needs that both the special procedures and the Human Rights Council currently have. This leads us to wonder if, just as a rationalization of the thematic and country mandates was considered necessary when the Council was created in 2006, another one may be necessary regarding the working methods of the Council, in order to allow UN experts and States to collaborate in a constructive and sufficient manner to come closer to achieving their basic objectives in their fields of work.[33]

If we add to this the need to follow-up on the recommendations not only at the intergovernmental level within the Human Rights Council, but also at the national level where their application could lead to a better an improved protection, promotion and respect of human rights, the task seems to be titanic for the special procedures, given their economic and human resources. The current organization of the Council and of special procedures points to the political will of States as the only option to achieve real change. Thus, international cooperation, as well as the cooperation between States and experts, is fundamental to achieve the objectives and commitments that at least theoretically all Member States have assumed, as well as to avoid projecting an image of diplomatic hypocrisy, where commitments are signed and responsibilities are taken without the necessary political will to implement them in practice.

Another difficulty that UN Special Rapporteurs, Independent Experts and Working Groups face is related to the reparations owed to victims of human rights violations. Even if guidelines have been created within the UN on

---

33 "Most importantly, the Council needs to devote the time necessary for a proper consideration of the reports of the special procedures and for proper follow-up. Failure to do so was one of the biggest failings of the previous system." *Id.*, at 19. Kothari argues that "Interaction of the SPs with the Council is limited and there is a need to increase the time given for such interaction. In the same spirit, the Council needs to provide greater support to SPs in adopting their recommendations. The council and OHCHR also need to institutionalize a mechanism to follow-up the recommendations made in the SPs' thematic and country reports. Follow-up to the work of the SPs, as well as that of treaty bodies and the UPR recommendations, remains a major weakness of the UN human rights system." See M. KOTHARI, above n 29, at 614–615.

the reparations of grave human rights violations or of serious breaches of international humanitarian law (the *van Boven Principles*),[34] which should guide States on the form that reparations should take, in many occasions it is necessary to have qualified advice that facilitates the elaboration and adoption of such measures.

Additionally, it is necessary that special procedures take into consideration the right to reparation as one of the main standards of international human rights law, so that they systematically suggest to States specific forms of reparation whenever a human rights violation has taken place, particularly where victims have not been compensated or awarded an integral reparation.[35] This function is essential to have more certainty regarding the actions the State must take in response to allegation letters sent to the Office of the High Commissioner for Human Rights against it, for it renders the form and procedures to be undertaken more visible and doesn't leave the adoption of measures of protection and non-repetition to the interpretation of the State.

The adoption of a UN policy on early response to potential crisis situations is also necessary, and it's a field where special procedures can use their allegation letters and urgent appeals procedures. Just as urgent appeals have a preventive character, this policy should be oriented to avoiding a lack of action whenever trustworthy information on tendencies or recent events that could potentially lead to a human rights crisis are known.[36]

The activity of the Special Procedures is fundamental for the work carried out by the Human Rights Council, given that without UN human rights experts and their work of monitoring and response to allegations of human rights violations around the world, the United Nations would see their possibilities of protecting human rights very limited.[37] Through their work in developing and consolidating international human rights law,

---

34 General Assembly, *Basic Principles and Guidelines on the Right to a Remedy and Reparation for Victims of Gross Violations of International Human Rights Law and Serious Violations of International Humanitarian Law*, A/RES/60/147 (16 December 2005).

35 For further reference, see I. NIFOSI-SUTTEN, above n 22, at 409–410.

36 See J. GUTTER, above n 14, at 103; I. NIFOSI-SUTTEN, above n 22, at 410.

37 P. SCANNELLA and P. SPLINTER, 'The United Nations Human Rights Council: A Promise to Be Fulfilled' (2007) 7:1 *HRLR* 41, 59.

in supervising the respect and application of the necessary standards to ensure the efficacy of human rights, and thanks to their quasi-jurisdictional function through its complaints mechanisms, the special procedures have evolved to become into one of the most flexible, innovative and more responsive tools in the international machinery for the protection of human rights.[38] Even if there is still much left to do and they face many challenges, it is also true that the contribution made by special procedures has been necessary to reinforce the place of human rights under international law.

It is necessary that the system of special procedures collaborate closely with the other existing mechanisms under international human rights law, particularly with Treaty Bodies and the Universal Periodic Review, in order to reinforce its influence and effects in the protection of human rights. The analysis of the interaction between Special Procedures and Treaty Bodies is beyond the scope of this article;[39] however, the next section will discuss the Universal Periodic Review, analyzing the areas where these two procedures of the UN Human Rights Council could collaborate more closely.

IV. THE UNIVERSAL PERIODIC REVIEW

The Universal Periodic Review (UPR) was conceived as the banner that would distance the Human Rights Council from the politicization, subjectivity and selectivity that characterized the Commission on Human Rights during its last years. Through this mechanism, States would finally have a non-politicized tool that allowed them to evaluate globally the state of human rights in all UN Member States.[40] Thus, resolution A/RES/60/251 of the General Assembly determined in its paragraph 5.e) that:

---

38 T. BALDWIN-PASK and P. SCANNELLA, above n 30, at 421.

39 It must be mentioned that, contrary to Treaty Bodies, whose action is limited to those countries that have ratified the conventions creating them, one of the advantages of thematic Special Procedures is that they can assess human rights violations within their mandate wherever they occur, regardless of the existence of a ratification, which gives them wide capacities for investigation. *Id.*, at 420.

40 "Under this new mechanism, the Council will review the fulfillment of the human rights obligations and commitments by all Member States of the United Nations. Thus it aims to address the former Commission's lack of objectivity and impartiality in dealing with country situations…" See C. CALLEJÓN, above n 24, at 334. De La Vega and Lewis share the same vision, considering that the Universal Periodic Review was the result of an emerging ideology according to which the

> *5. Decides that the Council shall, inter alia:*
>
> ...
>
> *e) Undertake a universal periodic review, based on objective and reliable information, on the fulfillment by each State of its human rights obligations and commitments in a manner which ensures universality of coverage and equal treatment with respect to all States; the review shall be a cooperative mechanism, based on an interactive dialogue, with the full involvement of the country concerned and with consideration given to its capacity-building needs; such a mechanism shall complement and not duplicate the work of treaty bodies; the Council shall develop the modalities and necessary time allocation for the universal periodic review mechanism within one year after the holding of its first session;*

A universal monitoring and overview mechanism on the state of human rights at the global level was established, with the purpose of achieving an international cooperation in the field that would allow countries to individually determine their weaknesses, receive external criticisms regarding their performance, and receive recommendations from other countries in the world on how to improve the human rights situation in their country.[41] It was conceived as an effective mechanism that would prevent States from shielding or hiding themselves behind the political or regional blocs that supported each other, as it was the case during the existence of the Commission on Human Rights.[42]

The Universal Periodic Review started to function in 2008, through the annual examination of 48 UN Member States regarding the human rights situation in their country; its main goal was to promote the respect

---

integral human rights record of every country should be a part to an international discourse on human rights. See C. DE LA VEGA and T.N. LEWIS, 'Peer Review in the Mix: How the UPR Transforms Human Rights Discourse' in M.C. BASSIOUNI and W.A. SCHABAS (eds.), *New Challenges for the UN Human Rights Machinery. What Future for the UN Treaty Body System and the Human Rights Council Procedures?*, Intersentia, Cambridge 2011, p. 353.

41 "...in the context of the UPR, peer review should be viewed as a mechanism to assist countries in identifying undesirable practices in their internal human rights situations and finding ways to rectify violations of human rights through interaction with fellow member states." C. DE LA VEGA and T.N. LEWIS, above n 40, at 363.

42 "The UPR, it's a fact, formally gives no room for selectivity, as the review program is systematic and does not reflect the concerns of particular States or groups of States at a certain moment." O. DE FROUVILLE, above n 19, at 250.

of human rights through peer-review and feedback, as well as through feedback provided by other international stakeholders.[43] Thus, the UPR sought that the feedback (and therefore the pressure) between countries in the human rights field remains an inter-State matter, for it would theoretically allow for more attention devoted to such issues than if it came only from its interior.

Its methods of work are originally established in resolution 5/1 of the Human Rights Council, related to the institution-building package of the organ, dated 18 June 2007.[44] This document determined that the Universal Periodic Review would evaluate the performance of States regarding their respect and compliance with the UN Charter, the Universal Declaration of Human Rights, the international human rights instruments ratified by each country, the promises and voluntary pledges (even those undertaken jointly during a campaign to obtain a seat in the Council), and where applicable, of international humanitarian law. This way, taking into account the cyclic and permanent work that the UPR would imply, it was initially determined that the first cycle would last four years, where the human rights performance of 48 States per year would be examined during three annual sessions, each with a duration of two weeks.

For the evaluation, the State under review must present a national report on its human rights commitments, as well as on the form and actions adopted for its compliance; in the meantime, the Office of the High Commissioner for Human Rights makes a report on the observations made to that State by Treaty Bodies and the Special Procedures System, as well as a second report on reliable information from other stakeholders, such as academics, NGOs or national human rights institutions.

The process foresees the conformation of a Working Group on the Universal Periodic Review that includes the President of the Human Rights Council and delegations of the 47 Member States to the Council. Once

43 E.R. McMAHON, *The Universal Periodic Review: A Work in Progress*, Friedrich Ebert Stiftung, Berlin 2012, p. 4.

44 The original procedure was established in resolution A/HRC/RES/5/1; however, it was slightly reformed by resolution A/HRC/RES/16/21 of 12 April 2011, where the work and functioning of the Human Rights Council was reviewed, in accordance with General Assembly resolution A/RES/60/251. This resolution set forth the creation of the Council, and also its review five years after it began its operations. We will review the slight modifications made to the UPR in the following paragraphs.

the corresponding reports have been delivered, three rapporteurs from the Member States are chosen by the drawing of lots, conforming a *troika* that is in charge of preparing the report of the State under review, and of transmitting the questions formulated by other countries prior to the review.

The State under review must present its national report to the Working Group, after which the remaining States of the Council have the opportunity to initiate an interactive dialogue, where States generally commend, reproach or make recommendations regarding actions adopted by the State under review to strengthen their internal system of promotion and respect of human rights. The Working Group must include in its report on the review of the State a summary of the proceedings, the conclusions and/or recommendations, and the voluntary commitments adopted by the State after its review. Once the State has communicated to the Working Group its decision regarding the recommendations under consideration, the Plenary of the Human Rights Council will be in a position to adopt the final result.

In compliance with the mandate set forth in resolution 60/251, once the first ten sessions of the Working Group on the Universal Periodic Review passed, the Human Rights Council presented resolution A/HRC/16/21 of 12 April 2011 to the General Assembly. This resolution served for the Council to present the outcome of its internal review, formalizing several modifications to its work and mechanisms, including to the Universal Periodic Review.[45] Therefore, between the tenth and eleventh sessions of the Working Group on the UPR (that is, towards the end of the first UPR cycle, which had 12 sessions), the Council determined to introduce several changes to its functioning in order to improve the evaluation of States under review, which were intended to enter into force in the second cycle of the Universal Periodic Review.

Among the reforms and decisions adopted in the resolution, the Council determined that the second cycle of the UPR would start in June 2012 and that it would have a four-and-a-half-years periodicity, where it would review 42 States instead of the 48 reviewed per year during the first cycle. Thus, for every session after the second cycle, the Working Group would review 14 States instead of 16. In addition, one of the most important

45 Human Rights Council, *Review of the work and functioning of the Human Rights Council*, Res. A/HRC/RES/16/21 (12 April 2011), and its Annex, *Outcome of the review of the work and functioning of the United Nations Human Rights Council.*

reforms to the mechanism determined to encourage the participation of other stakeholders, including national human rights institutions, in order to broaden their participation in the review of States and have a national source of information that at least theoretically would be independent. Thus, paragraph 9 of the Annex determined that NHRIs that contribute information to the mechanism would have a separate section in the stakeholders' report, while paragraph 13 set forth that NHRIs would be entitled to intervene immediately after the State under review during the interactive dialogue.

Another significant change that points to one of the main obstacles faced by the UN human rights system is related to the position of the State and the follow-up given to the recommendations received. One of the reforms included in the outcome of the review of the work and functioning of the Human Rights Council is that the State under review must inform in writing to the Council on its position regarding all the recommendations received; thus, the basis of the follow-up would focus on the accepted recommendations, which already started in the second cycle.

On the follow-up, the resolution determined that States would have the opportunity to present a voluntary mid-term report, which should contain information on the follow-up measures adopted in relation to the recommendations that were accepted by the State under review in the prior cycle. It would have been convenient that the mid-term report was mandatory; however, State practice could eventually turn this voluntary contribution into a customary practice that would help to consolidate the presentation of reports in the human rights field.

At the time of writing, 126 States have been reviewed in the second cycle during the 13th to 21st sessions of the Working Group; thus, implementation of the aforementioned reforms has already taken place. We recently mentioned that follow-up measures are one of the main obstacles for the UN human rights system. This has been demonstrated in the activities of Special Procedures and Treaty Bodies. For the Universal Periodic Review, this is its most important test, for its success or failure depends on the effective implementation of the recommendations that have been accepted by States.[46]

[46] In the opinion of De Frouville, the follow-up given to recommendations made during the first cycle will determine whether the UPR has been a successful tool. See O. DE FROUVILLE, above n 19, at 250. De la Vega and Lewis consider that

Several criticisms have appeared regarding the Universal Periodic Review, despite its first phase still being underway, given that the completion of the first and second cycles would allow measuring the global results more comprehensively. One of them is worth mentioning: the success in the promotion, protection and respect of human rights, at least since 1993, has been the result of their indivisible and interrelated character, which has allowed for important case-law, political, and scientific developments. However, despite this publicized characteristic, the indivisibility and interrelatedness of human rights has not yet translated to its organic structures – especially to Special Procedures and Treaty Bodies –, which continue to work separately and independently. Even if some outreach has existed in specific areas (for example, in the case of the Working Group and the Committee on Enforced Disappearances), there has not been a definite organizational culture that leads to unity in the different processes. This may have limited the development of a holistic perspective in the UN human rights system.[47]

Thus, one of the main areas of opportunity for the stalwart mechanism of the Human Rights Council lies precisely in that complementary character. Even if since its conception the UPR was designed as a mechanism that should be complementary in order to avoid duplication of the work undertaken by already-existing procedures, it is necessary for its influence to grow in order to obtain real and effective commitments from States, so that they actually follow-up and apply the recommendations made by the different Council's procedures.[48]

---

a successful follow-up phase will be what determines if the UPR is an effective mechanism for bringing changes to the human rights situations of countries. See C. DE LA VEGA and T.N. LEWIS, above n 40, at 383.

47 Sweeney and Saito disagree with this position, pointing that the UPR has complemented the work carried out by Treaty Bodies by encouraging States to comply with their procedural obligations (that is, with the presentation of reports to the corresponding committees), as well as through interim follow-up measures to substantive issues raised by Treaty Bodies. See G. SWEENEY and Y. SAITO, 'An NGO Assessment of the New Mechanisms of the UN Human Rights Council' (2009) 9:2 *HRLR* 203, 213–214. However, it is necessary to have a closer coordination and collaboration between the different bodies and UN agencies.

48 De Frouville argues that there is no complementarity, given that there is no real interaction between the Universal Periodic Review and other human rights mechanisms, and that the UPR tends to cast a shadow over them. See O. DE FROUVILLE, above n 19, at 250–252. Sweeney and Saito also mention that despite some difficult questions asked in most sessions during the first cycle of the UPR,

The evaluation of States in accordance with the wide provisions of resolution 5/1 allows taking into consideration achievements regarding all human rights, even those protected not only by the UN Charter and the Universal Declaration of Human Rights, but also by international human rights treaties ratified by them. Therefore, a more complete global monitoring will exist regarding issues pertaining, for example, to the competence of the Human Rights Committee, to the Committee for the Elimination of Racial Discrimination or to the Committee on Economic, Social and Cultural Rights; in this sense, the Universal Periodic Review will undoubtedly become another front from which international pressure on States to comply with their international obligations and commitments will take place.[49]

Furthermore, the success of this new mechanism depends largely on the goodwill of States to undertake the necessary domestic processes in order to implement the accepted recommendations. Even if at the domestic level of every country there are specific procedures and situations pertaining to the political and socio-economic context that would allow the implementation of the recommendations made by the UPR, the ratification of the different human rights treaties imposes on States the duty to harmonize its domestic

---

the recommendations were generally so broad that it was practically impossible to monitor their implementation. See G. SWEENEY and Y. SAITO, above n 47, at 212. Due to this, in order to avoid or reduce the lack of clarity and redundancy on the recommendations issued, it would be wise to group them by theme and to impose a temporal limit to their implementation, so that they can be measured more easily. In addition, the references to Treaty Bodies and Special Procedures in the context of the UPR serve as a follow-up mechanism to the recommendations and observations made by the different committees and independent experts, which helps to highlight their significance and to strengthen human rights procedures. See C. DE LA VEGA and T.N. LEWIS, above n 40, at 372, 378–383.

49 Avoiding duplication of work has been one of the main concerns in the field of human rights, especially after the start of operation of the Universal Periodic Review. However, as stated by the Canadian delegation during the *travaux préparatoires* of the mechanism, peer-review should focus on the implementation of recommendations received to avoid duplication of work, and build upon the basis of existing information (presented by Treaty Bodies or Special Procedures) instead of requesting the presentation of new information. In addition, the facts that States commit to have a periodic interactive dialogue and that all States have an obligation to participate in this exercise are factors that demonstrate the complementary character of the mechanism, instead of a duplication of functions. See F.D. GAER, 'A Voice Not An Echo: Universal Periodic Review and the UN Treaty Body System' (2007) 7:1 *HRLR* 109, 114–115.

legislation with international standards, in order to avoid a normative polarization that could eventually lead to a violation of international law. The universal character of the new mechanism of the Human Rights Council can therefore contribute to the development of a universal awareness regarding the duty to harmonize the domestic legal order with its international counterpart, in order to comply with the State's international obligations and promote respect of human rights.[50]

The Universal Periodic Review may serve (and should be considered) as an instrument within an intergovernmental process aiming for the monitoring of the implementation of recommendations and decisions adopted by independent experts within the UN human rights system.[51] Even if the political character of the Human Rights Council will not be eradicated[52] given its intergovernmental nature, this should not be a legitimate impediment for its success or that of the UPR, as long as the necessary progress that confirms the imperative character of respecting human rights worldwide is achieved.

V. CONCLUDING THOUGHTS

International human rights law requires State cooperation in the adoption of reforms, mechanisms and national structures that allow individuals and groups to enjoy their human rights, and States to ensure it, in order to comply with their international obligations. In this sense, the UN Human Rights Council is a universal platform where the representation of

---

50 "The UPR could in fact provide added value and complement the treaty bodies in that its review of human rights compliance could be universal, covering every state in turn – which has not been the case for the treaty bodies, at least not yet." *Id.*, at 136.

51 O. DE FROUVILLE, above n 19, at 261. In the same sense, see E.R. McMAHON, above n 43, at 10, who considers that in principle, the objective of the Universal Periodic Review consists in ensuring that all countries are accountable for the progress or lack of regarding the implementation of recommendations.

52 O. DE FROUVILLE, above n 19, at 244. Pinheiro agrees, by mentioning that taking into consideration that the Commission (and currently the Council) was a multilateral political body integrated by State representatives who participated to defend their interests, it is hard to deny the political nature of these organs, being an intrinsic characteristics of their functioning. See P.S. PINHEIRO, above n 27, at 108–109.

different cultures, lifestyles and political, cultural and religious orientations converge, in order to share good practices and experiences that are useful for the development of programs and policies that favor the most disadvantaged. Also, this intergovernmental forum has achieved important progress for the international human rights system in its first nine years, on issues such as enforced disappearances, indigenous peoples' rights, extreme poverty or the effect of corporate activities on human rights, among many others.

A broad cooperation from States is necessary to ensure the appropriate functioning of the international machinery that protects human rights, both at the regional and universal level. This includes financial contributions that provide sufficient funds to the actions and campaigns undertaken by international organizations; it also involves cooperation in the implementation of recommendations and international norms; and particularly, that cooperation should be based on a genuine belief on the activities that are undertaken, in order to grant legitimacy to the intergovernmental process that defines the future actions and direction of the international organization. These three characteristics are necessary if the Human Rights Council, and particularly the Special Procedures and Universal Periodic Review, are to succeed in their objective to develop, promote and protect human rights around the world.

THE DOMESTIC IMPLEMENTATION OF THE RIGHT TO FOOD IN LATIN AMERICA AND THE CARIBBEAN

Olivier De Schutter*

I. INTRODUCTION

The effective implementation of the right to food is one of the main challenges of the twenty-first century for governments worldwide, given the need to design strategies and implement human and financial resources to ensure its protection. Thus, an important effort is necessary to effectively guarantee one of the essential components of the right to health, which in addition to the right to water and its sanitation is necessary to live a life in dignity.[1]

---

* Member of the UN Committee on Economic, Social and Cultural Rights; former UN Special Rapporteur on the right to food (2008–2014). Professor at the University of Louvain. I wish to thank Humberto Cantú Rivera for his editing and translation of this article from its original in Spanish.

1 The right to adequate food is recognized in Article 25 of the Universal Declaration of Human Rights, in Article 11 of the International Covenant on Economic, Social and Cultural Rights, interpreted by the Committee on Economic, Social and Cultural Rights in its General Comment N° 12, as well as in other international and regional human rights instruments, such as the Convention on the Rights of the Child (Arts. 24 and 27), the Convention on the Elimination of All Forms of Discrimination against Women (Arts. 12 and 14) or the Convention on the Rights of Persons with Disabilities (Arts. 25 and 28). Furthermore, the International Covenant on Civil and Political Rights covers some aspects of the right to food, particularly under article 6 (right to life). As the Human Rights Committee underlines, the right to life, among other things, demands that States adopt all possible measures to eliminate malnutrition. At the regional level, the right to food is enshrined in article 12 of the Additional Protocol to the American Convention on Human Rights in the Area of Economic, Social and Cultural Rights (the "Protocol of San Salvador") of 1988. For the interpretations made by human rights treaty bodies, see UN Committee on Economic, Social and Cultural Rights, *General Comment No. 12: The right to adequate food (Art. 11)*, E/C.12/1999/5 (12 May 1999); UN Human Rights Committee, *General Comment N° 6: Article 6 (Right to Life)*, HRI/GEN/1/Rev.9 (Vol. 1) (30 April 1982), par. 5.

This challenge is more intense in developing countries. The food crisis – which itself represents the worst violation of the human right to food – is the result of decisions and public policies made in the past based on wrong diagnostics, which were unfortunately addressed with ineffective or insufficient methods. One of the main causes of this socio-economic phenomenon was the scarce investment in the agricultural sector, or investments in agricultural projects that were inappropriate, and which were therefore insufficient to reduce or combat poverty. Likewise, macroeconomic policies in the agricultural sector diminished both nationally and internationally, which then made public and private investments focus on other areas.[2]

In line with their sovereign commitments to international or regional human rights instruments (such as the International Covenant on Economic, Social and Cultural Rights or in the Latin American context, the American Convention on Human Rights and its Optional Protocol), States have a duty to respect, protect and fulfill human rights. To achieve this triptych, they must implement appropriate public policies to ensure effective compliance with their international human rights obligations in order to protect their population, especially those in a situation of vulnerability.

Latin American and Caribbean countries are spearheading efforts to include within their legal and regulatory frameworks the right to food, as well as in adopting public policies and programs aimed at fighting hunger and food insecurity. Heads of State and Governments in Latin America and the Caribbean have reaffirmed in several occasions their commitment to prioritize the fight against food and nutritional insecurity, and to build the foundation of those efforts on the right to food.[3]

Congressmen and national parliaments have played an active role in positioning the right to food at the highest level of political agendas in

---

2 O. DE SCHUTTER and K.Y. CORDES, 'Accounting for Hunger: An Introduction to the Issues' in O. DE SCHUTTER and K.Y. CORDES (eds.), *Accounting for Hunger: The Right to Food in the Era of Globalisation*, Oxford University Press, Oxford 2011, pp. 2–4.

3 An example is the *Declaration of Salvador de Bahia*, adopted in the first Latin America and Caribbean Summit on Integration and Development in December 2008. A similar commitment exists in the *Iniciativa América Latina y Caribe Sin Hambre*, launched by the President of Guatemala Oscar Berger and the President of Brazil Lula Da Silva in 2005, with the goal of eradicating hunger in the region by year 2025. See www.ialcsh.org/es (last accessed on 10 February 2015).

the region. A *Parliamentarian Front against Hunger in Latin America and the Caribbean* (FPH) was established in September 2009. It is organized at national, sub-regional and inter-American levels and has as its mission promoting legislation and legal frameworks that recognize and guarantee the right to food.[4] Also in 2009, the Latin American Parliament adopted the *Latin American Declaration on Human Rights*, which included the right to food in its article 11.[5]

Nevertheless, despite the progress achieved, the right to food is still unfulfilled for a large proportion of people living in Latin America and the Caribbean. As it has happened in other regions around the world, the combined effects of the world food crisis and the economic crisis of 2007–2009 gravely affected the access to adequate food, and largely dismantled the progress achieved during the last 15 years to fight hunger and reduce food and nutritional insecurity. While the poverty rate in the region started to decline again in 2010, an estimated 12 percent of population in the region (70 million people) is still living under extreme poverty conditions and have no access to a basic food basket. Besides, the situation for the poorer and more food-insecure population doesn't seem to have improved in 2011 and could even have worsened, since the positive effect of increased household income has been limited by the increase in food prices.[6]

As elsewhere around the world, most people in the region that suffer from food insecurity live in rural areas where food is produced, and yet they buy food instead of selling it.[7] This happens despite the exponential increase that agricultural production has experienced in the last few years in Latin America and the Caribbean. As shown by recent studies, the main reason why this incremented agricultural production has not implied a reduction in rural poverty and food insecurity is that the development has taken place

---

4 Parliamentarian fronts are being established at the national level more often. Only in 2011, national parliamentarian fronts were established in Argentina, Colombia, Dominican Republic, Ecuador, Honduras, Mexico, Nicaragua, Paraguay and Uruguay. It was established before in Brazil.

5 Adopted in Panama in December 2009 during the *XXV Ordinary Session of the Latin-American Parliament*, convened in Panama City on the 3rd of December of 2009. Article 11 sets forth that: "Latin Americans have the right to a food that ensures a healthy physical and mental development".

6 ECLAC, *Social panorama of Latin America 2011,* United Nations and ECLAC, Santiago 2011, p.4.

7 The World Bank, *World Development Report 2008. Agriculture for Development*, The World Bank, Washington DC 2008, p. 95.

in very few regions within each country, and has been limited to specific products and to large and medium-sized producers with access to external markets.[8] The increase in agricultural production underlines the fact that it is not a lack of food availability that limits the effective implementation of the right to food for everyone in the region. Rather, the main challenge lies in ensuring that food production methods and systems allow people in urban and rural areas to have access to adequate food.

This article will analyze the importance of the right to food, as well as the need for its protection by national constitutions in order for it to be recognized as one of the rights with a higher hierarchy and importance for the life and well being of the population. In the same sense, its harmonization through secondary laws, national strategies and public policies will be reviewed. A special focus on some of the essential characteristics for the implementation of this right, such as monitoring and accountability, and its effective implementation in a multisectoral and participative manner will also be discussed. Finally, we will emphasize the main results and conclusions obtained from the analysis of legal standards and public policies in Latin America and the Caribbean on the issue of food and nutritional security, and therefore in the progressive implementation of the human right to food in the region.

II. THE IMPORTANCE OF THE RIGHT TO ADEQUATE FOOD

The right to food can be summarized as the human right to be able to feed oneself with dignity, either through food production or acquisition. As the UN Committee on Economic, Social and Cultural Rights has stated, the right "is realized when every man, woman and child, alone or in community with others, have physical and economic access at all times to adequate food or means for its procurement."[9]

---

8 J.G. DA SILVA, S. GOMEZ and R. CASTAÑEDA (eds.), *Boom agrícola y persistencia de la pobreza rural: Estudio de ocho casos*, FAO, Santiago 2009, available at www.fao.org/alc/file/media/pubs/2009/boomagri.pdf (last accessed on 10 February 2015). The report is based on the results of eight case studies from Argentina, Brazil, Chile, Colombia, Guatemala, Mexico, Nicaragua and Peru.

9 UN Committee on Economic, Social and Cultural Rights, *General Comment No. 12: The right to adequate food (Art. 11)*, E/C.12/1999/5 (12 May 1999), par. 6.

The normative and analytic framework of the right to food underlines the importance of political will, empowerment and the participation of civil society, accountability mechanisms and progress-monitoring undertaken in the application of multi-annual strategies. As Amartya Sen stated, "The law is between food availability and the right to food."[10] This means that unless we take seriously our duties to those that are more vulnerable and the essential role of legal remedies to ensure that poor people have the necessary resources to produce enough food for themselves or a sufficient purchasing power to acquire food, efforts to increase food production will have little effect. Why are they hungry? It's not because there is scarce food, but because they are economically marginalized and politically impotent. Protecting the right to food through adequate institutions and monitoring mechanisms must therefore be a fundamental part of any strategy against hunger.

The growing recognition of the importance and usefulness of a legal and regulatory framework on the right to food reflects a growing understanding that hunger is not just a supply-and-demand problem, but mainly a problem of a lack of access to productive resources like land and water, of a supplier sector that is more and more concentrated, and of insufficient social security networks to support the poor. It is well known by governments, civil society and social movements that the right to food constitutes a tool to improve the efficacy of policies that aim to combat hunger and malnutrition. They understand the importance of a major equity in food supply chains, of empowerment and accountability, and of the need to devote more attention to the power inequities in the food systems and to the lack of support for small-scale agricultural producers, which hinders their capacity to feed themselves, their families and their communities.

III. CONSTITUTIONAL PROTECTION OF THE RIGHT TO FOOD

The fact that the right to food is explicitly recognized in the domestic constitutions and legal frameworks of most Latin American and Caribbean countries constitutes evidence of the political will to ensure the effectiveness of this prerogative in the region. In this sense, Latin America and the

---

10 A. SEN, *Poverty and Famines: An Essay on Entitlement and* Deprivation, Oxford University Press, Oxford 1987, pp. 165–66.

Caribbean are heading a global trend.[11] At the present moment, a growing number of States around the globe (24 in total according to a recent survey) explicitly protect the right to food in their constitutions; 15 of them are among the 33 Latin America and Caribbean States.[12]

More recently, in October 2011 a process of constitutional reform was completed in Mexico, inserting the right to food in the Constitution through important changes in articles 4 and 27, setting forth that "every person has the right to nutritious, sufficient and quality food. The state shall guarantee such right" (article 4), and that "the integral and sustainable rural development (…) shall also have among its objectives that the State guarantees a sufficient and timely provision of the basic food that the law determines" (article 27).[13]

In El Salvador, in April 2012, the Legislative Assembly approved a constitutional reform to include the right to food. Through the reform to article 69, the Constitution now sets forth that "Every person has the right to adequate food. It is an obligation of the State to create a policy of nutrition and food security for all the residents. A law shall regulate this matter" (…) "the State shall control the quality of the food products and the environmental conditions that may affect the health and well-being."[14]

---

11 J.L. VIVERO POL and P. RAMIREZ, 'Leyes, políticas e instituciones contra el hambre en el contexto latinoamericano' in J.L. VIVERO and X. ERAZO (eds.), *Derecho a la Alimentación, Políticas Públicas e Instituciones contra el Hambre*, Ediciones LOM, Santiago 2009, p. 152, available at http://issuu.com/joseluisvivero/docs/cap_5_leyes_pol_ticas_e_instituciones_san_en_alc_v (last accessed on 10 February 2015).

12 L. KNUTH and M. VIDAR, *Constitutional and Legal Protection of the Right to Food Around the World*, FAO, Rome 2011, p. 13; and J. L. VIVERO POL and P. RAMIREZ, above n 11, at 152–153. Ten countries currently recognize the right to food as a specific right applicable to the whole population. The constitutions of ten other countries set forth the right to food for specific categories of the population, such as children or convicts. Five countries have constitutional provisions setting forth the right to food as a part of another human right.

13 The Special Rapporteur welcomed the adoption of new constitutional provisions in a press release issued on 13 October 2011, available at: www.ohchr.org/SP/NewsEvents/Pages/DisplayNews.aspx?NewsID=11491&LangID=S (last accessed on 10 February 2015).

14 The reform (in August 2012) still had to be ratified by the new Assembly to enter into force.

Similar provisions that explicitly guarantee the right to food as a general right for all can be found in the constitutions of Bolivia, Brazil, Ecuador, Guatemala, Guyana, Haiti and Nicaragua.[15] In other four countries in the region, national constitutions guarantee the right to food for specific groups, for example "the right to food of children" in the constitutions of Colombia (art. 44), Cuba (art. 9) and Honduras (arts. 142–146); or the right to food is mentioned in the context of the right to work, such as in the Constitution of Suriname (art. 24). Finally, three constitutions implicitly guarantee the right to food by elevating the International Covenant on Economic, Social and Cultural Rights and other international human rights treaties ratified by the State to the constitutional or *supra*-constitutional level (such is the case of Argentina, El Salvador and Costa Rica).

Constitutional amendments to recognize the right to food that have been done or that are under consideration throughout the region are in line with the recommendations of the Voluntary Guidelines to support the progressive realization of the right to adequate food in the context of national food security (hereinafter "FAO Guidelines").[16] Thus, Guideline 7 refers that "States are invited to consider, in accordance with their domestic legal and policy frameworks, whether to include provisions in their domestic law, possibly including constitutional or legislative review that facilitates the progressive realization of the right to adequate food in the context of national food security."

Civil society and social movements have been crucial to promote the inclusion of the right to food in national constitutions. In the case of Mexico, the constitutional reform approved in October 2011 was the result of twenty years of promotion and lobbying by civil society groups. These efforts began in 1992, when 30 civil society organizations created the "Front for the Right to Food" (*Frente por el Derecho a la alimentación*), which filed a petition to the Chamber of Deputies for the constitutional recognition of the right to food.

15 Respectively in article 16 (Bolivia), article 10 (Brazil), article 13 (Ecuador), article 99 (Guatemala), article 40 (Guyana), article 22 (Haiti) and article 63 (Nicaragua).

16 The Guidelines were adopted by 187 Member States of the FAO Council in November 2004, available at www.fao.org/3/a-y7937e.pdf (last accessed on 10 February 2015).

In the case of Brazil, the proposal that derived in the 2010 constitutional amendment recognizing the right to food was initially presented by a member of Parliament in 2003, and later promoted by the President of the National Parliamentary Front on food and nutrition security, Mr. Nazareno Fonteles, with the support of different civil society organizations, including FIAN-Brazil, who collected more than 50,000 signatures of support to the constitutional amendment.

National human rights institutions have also played a very active role in some countries. For example, the Attorney General for the Defense of Human Rights of El Salvador presented a proposal in 2009 to include in the Constitution the right to food among the fundamental rights that shall be guaranteed to every person.

IV. LEGAL FRAMEWORKS

Even though the progress achieved in the explicit recognition of the right to food in national constitutions is very important, constitutional provisions alone are not sufficient. Generally speaking, the development of secondary laws and regulations that define in a detailed manner the mechanisms and responsibilities to make the right to food effective in practice is needed; this includes the monitoring mechanisms and legal and administrative remedies in case a violation of this right occurs. Important progress has also been noted in this regard within Latin America and the Caribbean.

In the last decade, laws on nutrition and food security (NFS) based on the right to food have been adopted in Argentina in 2003 (*Ley Programa Nacional de Nutrición*), in Guatemala in 2005 (*Ley Sistema Nacional de Seguridad Alimentaria y Nutricional*), in Ecuador in 2006 (*Ley de Seguridad Alimentaria y Nutricional*, substituted in 2009 by the *Ley de Soberanía y Seguridad Alimentaria y Nutricional*), in Brazil in 2006 (*Ley Orgánica de Seguridad Alimentaria y Nutricional*), in Venezuela in 2008 (*Ley Orgánica de Seguridad y Soberanía Agroalimentaria*), in Nicaragua in 2009 (*Ley de Soberanía y Seguridad Alimentaria y Nutricional*), and in Honduras in 2011 (*Ley de Seguridad Alimentaria y Nutricional*). Similar laws are currently under consideration by the respective parliaments of ten other countries in the region.[17] On the other hand, while a federal NFS bill is currently being studied in Mexico, the Legislative Assembly of Mexico City approved a NFS Law in 2009, the first of its kind in the country.

National NFS laws (and those at the state level) that are currently in force, as well as most of the ten bills that are currently under consideration, explicitly recognize the right to food as a central component of policies and national programs. For example, the NFS Law of Honduras (Decree No. 25–2011) specifies in its article 3 that respect for human rights is a key axis of the NFS policy, and that under the Law no person or group of persons can be discriminated, "especially in their right to produce, obtain, dispose and access to sufficient nutritious food."

Similarly to the promotion of the constitutional recognition of the right to food, the elaboration of NFS laws has been driven by the combined efforts of civil society, social movements, parliamentarians and national human rights institutions. The United Nations system has also provided support and advice in the elaboration of these laws, particularly FAO through its support to the *Hunger-Free Latin America and the Caribbean Initiative*[18] and the Team on the Right to Food in Rome, as well as the UN High Commissioner for Human Rights (OHCHR), through its national and sub-regional offices.

In particular, the notable growth of NFS laws based on the right to food has been driven by the dedication and commitment of parliamentarians, many of which are connected through the *Parliamentary Front Against Hunger*,[19] which serves as a network for sharing best practices among national parliaments to encourage the drafting and approval of laws that improve the protection of the right to food.

17 In Costa Rica, Colombia, Bolivia, El Salvador, Haiti, Mexico, Panama, Paraguay, Peru and the Dominican Republic.

18 The Hunger-Free Latin America and the Caribbean Initiative is supported by the FAO with the financial support of Brazil, Spain and other donors. For more information, see www.ialcsh.org/en/ (last accessed on 10 February 2015). A main objective of the Initiative is to raise social awareness on the right to food, including the preparation of national reports in cooperation with non-governmental organizations.

19 See above n 4.

V. NATIONAL STRATEGIES FOR THE REALIZATION OF THE RIGHT TO FOOD

Another important element of the domestic institutional frameworks for the protection of the right to food -besides constitutional protection and NFS laws- are national strategies and NFS plans of action that identify specific priorities and set concrete, measurable and time-framed goals for the progressive realization of the right to food.

In parallel to the progress in the field of constitutional reform and NFS legislation, a wide spectrum of national NFS strategies and plans of action has been developed in Latin America and the Caribbean in recent years, including *inter alia* the *Plan Nacional de Seguridad Alimentaria 2009–2015* of Paraguay, the *Política Nacional de Seguridad Alimentaria y Nutricional* of Nicaragua, the *Política de Seguridad Alimentaria y Nutricional 2006–2015* of Honduras, the *Política Nacional de Seguridad Alimentaria y Nutricional 2008* of Colombia, the *Estrategia Nacional de Reducción de la Desnutrición Crónica 2006–2016* of Guatemala, the *Política Nacional de Seguridad Alimentaria y Nutricional* (2003 and 2011) of El Salvador, and the *Plan Nacional de Seguridad Alimentaria y Nutricional 2009–2015* of Panama. Similarly, Brazil adopted in 2011 a National NFS Plan for 2012–2015, based on a human rights approach and involving seventeen ministries in the Inter-Ministerial Chamber of Nutrition and Food Security (CAISAN). This Plan sets forth a system of continuous monitoring and evaluation of the progressive realization of the human right to adequate food that uses benchmarks and information already used by sectorial systems, under the supervision of a technical committee involving multiple actors, including civil society representatives of CONSEA.[20]

A series of social programs at the national level are or have been in force in the fight against hunger and nutritional and food insecurity, such as the "*Fome Zero*" in Brazil, "*Vivir Mejor*" in Mexico, "*Bogotá Sin Hambre*" in Colombia, "*Desnutrición Cero*" in Bolivia, "*Hambre Cero*" in Guatemala or "*Hambre más urgente*" in Argentina.

---

20 CAISAN, *Plano Nacional de Segurança Alimentar e Nutricional: 2012/2015*, Brasilia 2011, available at www.mds.gov.br/segurancaalimentar/LIVRO_PLANO_NACIONAL_CAISAN_FINAL.pdf.pagespeed.ce.NSQXeyLv0S.pdf (last accessed on 10 February 2015).

The Committee on Economic, Social and Cultural Rights has insisted on the obligation of States, in accordance with the ICESCR, to work for the "adoption of a national strategy to ensure food and nutrition security for all, based on human rights principles that define the objectives, and the formulation of policies and corresponding benchmarks."[21] Guideline 3 of the FAO Guidelines also encourages the adoption of "a national human-rights based strategy for the progressive realization of the right to adequate food ... [that includes] objectives, targets, benchmarks and time frames; and actions to formulate policies, identify and mobilize resources, define institutional mechanisms, allocate responsibilities, coordinate the activities of different actors, and provide for monitoring mechanisms."

VI. KEY ELEMENTS OF NFS LAWS AND STRATEGIES BASED ON THE RIGHT TO FOOD

While most NFS laws and strategies refer to the realization of the right to adequate food as a central objective, the extent to which these laws and strategies are based on the human right to adequate food varies between countries.

From the standpoint of the right to food, national strategies must be based on the commitment of the State and its institutions and the national, regional and local/municipal level to realize the right to food, and must include the establishment of adequate institutional mechanisms to: (i) identify as soon as possible any emerging threats to the right to food, through adequate monitoring systems; (ii) improve accountability mechanisms, with a clear allocation of responsibilities and determination of fixed time frames to implement the dimensions of the right to food that require a progressive realization; (iii) improve the coordination between the different ministries, as well as between national and sub-national governmental institutions; (iv) ensure adequate participation, particularly of the groups most affected by food insecurity; (v) guarantee the political commitment and a sustainable financing for the effective application of laws, policies and strategies. As long as these conditions are not met, the different strategies adopted by governments may turn out to

21 UN Committee on Economic, Social and Cultural Rights, *General Comment No. 12: The right to adequate food (Art. 11)*, E/C.12/1999/5 (12 May 1999), par. 21.

be ineffective, due to the lack of a sanction for an inadequate or inexistent implementation.[22]

A. MONITORING AND ACCOUNTABILITY

The framework of the right to food requires that the establishment of goals and concrete measures is done through a consultative and transparent process with public participation; that the authorities in charge of its implementation are responsible of the results; and that the benchmarks to measure progress are based on the normative components of the right to food, including non-discrimination.

A basic requirement for the formulation of laws, policies and strategies for the realization of the right to adequate food is to have in place a system to collect relevant data on nutrition and food insecurity, and on the progress in the realization of the right to food. It is necessary that this data is collected in a way that allows for the identification of groups that are particularly vulnerable or disadvantaged. In this sense, the FAO Guidelines underscore the importance of systematically undertaking "disaggregated analysis on food insecurity, the vulnerability and nutritional situation of different groups of society" (Guideline 13,2).

Furthermore, there has to be a system to analyze this information and its relation with the application of laws, policies and strategies. Such periodical oversight must serve as a basis to review, and when necessary adjust, the policies and strategies to advance in the effective realization of the right to food.

While existing NFS systems in Latin America and the Caribbean establish several systems of data collection, they often don't provide sufficient

---

22 On the national strategies and opportunities for empowerment, participation and accountability, see FAO, *El derecho a la alimentación en la práctica. Aplicación a nivel nacional*, FAO, Rome 2011; FAO, *El derecho a la dependencia alimentaria*, FAO, Rome 2006; and the Special Rapporteur on the right to food, Olivier De Schutter, *Nota Explicativa: Países que se enfrentan al hambre desde el enfoque del derecho a la alimentación. Progreso significativo en la implementación del derecho a la alimentación a escala nacional en África, América Latina y Asia Meridional*, May 2010, available at www.srfood.org/images/stories/pdf/otherdocuments/20100805_briefing_note_01_es.pdf.

information to effectively evaluate the progress in the implementation of the right to food. This is reflected in the reiterated concerns raised by the Committee on Economic, Social and Cultural Rights to States regarding the lack of detailed disaggregated data to efficiently evaluate the level of progress reached in the realization of the right to food and other economic, social and cultural rights.[23] The lack of adequate information to evaluate progress is also mentioned in the reports of the national human rights institutions of Guatemala and Colombia. Besides, the information on nutrition and food security is not always available publicly, a feature that is essential to allow for appropriate oversight by civil society organizations and other interested stakeholders.

In addition, the oversight mechanisms could be strengthened through a more systematic use of indicators and benchmarks based on human rights.[24] In this sense, the OHCHR has developed a conceptual and methodological framework of indicators on the promotion and effectiveness of human rights, together with lists of illustrative indicators, including on the right to food.[25] Also, the FAO Voluntary Guidelines provide guidance on the development and use of indicators for the oversight of the progressive realization of the right to food (see Guideline 17).

Finally, to ensure accountability, national NFS systems must include mechanisms that are independent from Government to supervise the application of policies and strategies, a task that could be entrusted to national human rights institutions. Parliamentarian commissions could also play an important role in ensuring such independent oversight. NFS laws of Nicaragua and Guatemala set forth that the Attorney General

---

23 See e.g. UN Committee on Economic, Social and Cultural Rights, *Concluding Observations of the CESCR on Uruguay*, E/C.12/URY/CO/3–4 (1 December 2010); and UN Committee on Economic, Social and Cultural Rights, *Concluding Observations of the CESCR on Colombia*, E/C.12/COL/CO/5 (7 June 2010).

24 For example, the Special Rapporteur on the right to food recommended that the information system on nutrition and food security set forth by the Nicaraguan law should be strengthened through the adoption of a unified system of indicators, objectives and references to monitor State compliance with its obligation to progressively realize the right to food. See Report of the Special Rapporteur on the right to food, *Mission to Nicaragua*, A/HRC/13/33/Add.5 (19 February 2010), par. 83 (d).

25 OHCHR, *Using indicators to promote and monitor the implementation of human rights*, HRI/MC/2008/3 (6 June 2008), p. 24.

for Human Rights must supervise and prepare periodic reports on the implementation of the NFS law. Nevertheless, there is no mechanism to ensure an appropriate follow-up to its conclusions and recommendations. The NFS law of Honduras establishes a Commission for the Oversight of Nutrition and Food Security (*Comisión de Vigilancia de Seguridad Alimentaria y Nutricional*) that includes the National Human Rights Commissioner (CONADEH) and the President of the Commission on Nutrition and Food Security of the National Congress. However, their mandate is limited to monitor the application of the evaluation and monitoring policies of the national NFS system.

Legal supervision

Ensuring accountability is one of the main reasons for which the right to food must be enshrined in national legislation. To be effective in ensuring accountability, laws have to be enforceable before independent judicial, quasi-judicial or administrative bodies. As the FAO Guidelines indicate: "States that have established a right to adequate food under their legal system should inform the general public of all available rights and remedies to which they are entitled" (Guideline 7).

The degree to which NFS laws in force or under consideration ensure the justiciability of the right to food and include accountability mechanisms varies greatly between countries. Despite the fact that laws refer to the right to food and to the principles of transparency and accountability, they give little detail on how that accountability must take place in practice. The laws in force in Mexico City, Ecuador and Nicaragua, as well as the bill under consideration in Paraguay, refer specifically to the justiciability of the right to food, while other laws (including those of Argentina, Brazil, Guatemala and Venezuela) don't make that reference. However, none of the laws establish judicial, quasi-judicial or administrative mechanisms before which claims could be filed in case of violations of the right.[26] Neither are established sanctions for non-compliance with national legislation. This is one of the shortcomings in NFS systems and legal frameworks.

26 J.L. VIVERO, 'El enfoque jurídico contra el hambre: el derecho a la alimentación y las leyes de seguridad alimentaria' in X. ERAZO, L. PAUTASSI and A. SANTOS (eds.), *Exigibilidad y realización de derechos sociales. Impacto en la política pública*, LOM Ediciones, Santiago 2010, p. 184.

Tribunals could play an important role in ensuring the effectiveness of the right to food; the Constitutional Court of Colombia and the tribunals of Argentina, Guatemala, Honduras and Paraguay have demonstrated this.[27] Nevertheless, despite the right to food being included in domestic laws and national constitutions, there are very few cases in which courts have based their judgments on the right to food. One of the few cases worth mentioning is a judgment by the Court of Appeals of San Pedro Sula, Honduras, that was in favor of an *amparo* claim to avoid the eviction of a group of farmers in an agrarian conflict. In its judgment, the Court recognizes the argument of the counsel to the farmers referring to the obligation of the State to protect the right to food, which made reference to the ICESCR and General Comment N° 7 (on forced evictions) of the Committee on Economic, Social and Cultural Rights.[28] Of note is also a recent case from Mexico, from March 2012, which makes reference to the right to food and the NFS law of Mexico City, where the judgment was in favor of ensuring the right to adequate food on the basis of an "*amparo* trial."[29]

A recurring problem is the lack of familiarity of judges and lawyers with the right to food and its justiciability, despite this right being explicitly enshrined in laws and national constitutions of their countries. Thus, further training and awareness among the members of the Judiciary seems necessary. In this regard, the regional office of OHCHR in Guatemala has recently provided training to judges and lawyers on the right to food. In

---

27 On the justiciability of the right to food and the role of courts, see C. COURTIS, 'The Right to Food as a Justiciable Right: Challenges and Strategies', (2007) 11 *Max Planck Yearbook of United Nations Law* 317; C. GOLAY, *Derecho a la alimentación y acceso a la justicia: Ejemplos a nivel nacional, regional e internacional*, FAO, Rome 2009; FIAN Internacional, *Promover el derecho a la alimentación adecuada a nivel nacional. Algunas lecciones aprendidas*, FIAN, Heidelberg 2009; J.L. VIVERO POL, 'Hunger for Justice in Latin America. The Justiciability of Social Rights in Hungry Democracies' in J.L. VIVERO POL and M.A. MARTÍN LÓPEZ (coords.), *New Challenges to the Right to Food*, CEHAP & Huygens Editorial, Cordoba/Barcelona 2011, available at http://issuu.com/joseluisvivero/docs/hunger_for_justice_in_latin_america_jlv_huygens_fi/1 (last accessed on 10 February 2015). For a commented list of cases in Latin America and the Caribbean, see also the website www.escr-net.org/.

28 J.L. VIVERO POL, V. SCHOLZ HOSS and J.C. GARCÍA CEBOLLA, 'La justiciabilidad del derecho a la alimentación en América Latina', *Documentos de trabajo: Iniciativa América Latina Sin Hambre*, Santiago 2009, pp. 21–22.

29 See J. ROBLES, 'Indigente gana amparo al GDF', *El Universal*, 27 March 2012, available at: www.eluniversal.com.mx/ciudad/110851.html (last accessed on 10 February 2015).

some cases, judges have begun to incorporate the right to food in their judgments after receiving specific training on this right. It also seems that younger generations of judges and lawyers are more willing to use human rights norms in their judgments.

Bar associations and human rights organizations (NGOs) need to file more strategic litigation claims in order to create more case law that would allow rights-holders to claim their rights. Civil society organizations play a crucial role in facilitating access to judicial remedy. Without their support, it is very unlikely that people suffering from nutrition and food insecurity – who are generally among the most vulnerable groups of society – can complain about their situation before the authorities. Colombia, Argentina and Mexico provide good examples where, through strategic litigation, symbolic cases that benefit the society as a whole have been won.

National human rights institutions

Many countries have established independent national human rights institutions in accordance with the Principles relating to the Status of National Institutions (the "Paris Principles") that were adopted by the General Assembly in 1993. These institutions supervise the compliance of the State with its international human rights obligations, and in some cases they can receive claims by affected individuals. Even though these institutions have traditionally focused on civil and political rights, they are currently paying more attention to economic, social and cultural rights. For example, three national human rights institutions (from Guatemala, El Salvador and Colombia) have issued reports on the right to food and the application of a national NFS policy. In Argentina, in response to the actions of the Ombudsman, the Supreme Court decided in September 2007 that the State and the Government of the Chaco province had an obligation to provide food and safe drinking water to the indigenous communities in Toba; in Brazil, the Public Prosecutor's Office is integrated by independent prosecutors who can demand accountability from public authorities in the implementation of programs related to food and nutrition. Also in Brazil, the National Council for the Defense of the Rights of the Human Being (CDDPH) supervises violations of the rights to food. Nevertheless, the CDDPH currently has a limited mandate, and its decisions are not legally binding.[30]

---

30 Brazil has recently committed to transform the CDDPH into a national human rights institution in conformity with the Principles relating to the Status of

The Human Rights Prosecutor's Office (PDH) in Guatemala has a specific mandate to oversee the application of the national NFS policy.[31] In its fourth monitoring report of 2011, entitled "*La muerte por hambre... también es un crimen*", the Prosecutor's Office mentions that "[n]either the recommendations of the PDH of the three previous reports, nor those of other institutions have been included in the plans and actions of the members of the [National Council for Food Security] CONASAN", and regrets the continuous problems related to the lack of coordination in policies and programs despite the efforts of CONASAN. The 2012 report that was recently published highlights the low level of budgetary allocations of national funds, and how the NFS Secretariat is mainly financed by external development aid funds (over 80%).[32]

In addition, as part of its duty to promote the defense of human rights, the Ombudsman of Colombia published its first report on the right to food in 2012. The report analyzes the measures adopted to make the right to food effective after the adoption of the new national NFS policy in 2008, and identifies as the main issues the lack of a legal framework on Nutrition and Food Security in the country, as well as the inexistence of a coherent and coordinated action between the authorities responsible for the food public policy.[33]

Human rights monitoring at the regional and global level

Finally, it is important to mention the role of the regional and global monitoring mechanisms. For example, at the regional level, the Inter-American Court of Human Rights has solved cases related to the right to

---

National Institutions ("Paris Principles", Resolution 48/134 of the General Assembly, annex). This new institution would receive the human, material and budgetary resources necessary for its operation. See the second national report of Brazil before the Universal Periodic Review Mechanism (UPR) of the United Nations Human Rights Council: Human Rights Council, *National report of Brazil*, A/HRC/WG.6/13/BRA/1 (7 March 2012).

31 In line with article 14, subsection (j) of the legislative decree 32-2005, the Attorney General issues annual reports with specific recommendations on the implementation of nutrition and food security policies and strategies, which are addressed to the National Council on Nutrition and Food Security.

32 Procuraduría de Derechos Humanos de Guatemala, *Seguridad Alimentaria y Nutricional: de la asistencia humanitaria a la erradicación de la pobreza*, 2012.

33 Defensoría del Pueblo de Colombia, *Primer Informe del Derecho Humano a la Alimentación*, 2012.

food. For example, the Court considered that the Paraguayan State had violated the right to life by not ensuring access to food, water and health services to 19 members of an extremely poor indigenous community, because "the authorities knew or should have known about the existence of a situation posing an immediate and certain risk to the life of an individual or of a group of individuals, and that the necessary measures were not adopted within the scope of their authority which could be reasonably expected to prevent or avoid such risk".[34] The case does not refer specifically to the right to food, which is not recognized as a legally enforceable right under the American Convention on Human Rights and its Additional Protocol in the Area of Economic, Social and Cultural Rights ("Protocol of San Salvador"), despite being included in article twelve of the latter. Instead, the case refers to the right to food indirectly, as an integral part of the right to a life in dignity and the right to life.

Regarding the global human rights monitoring mechanisms, most of the countries in the region have ratified the international human rights treaties that guarantee the right to food, particularly the International Covenant on Economic, Social and Cultural Rights (ICESCR). The periodic review of State reports by the bodies created as a result of the international human rights treaties, such as the Committee on Economic, Social and Cultural Rights, provide an important forum for public debate and self-assessment of each Government on the level of implementation of the right to food.

The international monitoring system is actively used by non-governmental organizations in the region to prepare "alternative reports", with the objective of complementing the official reports submitted by States to treaty bodies. To reinforce international monitoring, States are encouraged to accept the complaints mechanism established in the Optional Protocol to the ICESCR. Latin-American States are well represented among the States that have so far ratified or signed the Protocol, demonstrating the importance accorded to the right to food and other economic, social and cultural rights in the region.[35]

---

34 I/A Court H.R., *Case of the Sawhoyamaxa Indigenous Community v. Paraguay.* Merits, Reparations and Costs. Judgment of March 29, 2006. Series C No. 146, para. 155.

35 Until the 1st of July of 2012, the Optional Protocol has been ratified by eight States, four of which are from Latin America (Argentina, Bolivia, Ecuador and El Salvador), and signed by 32 other States, including six from the region (Chile,

The Special Procedures of the UN Human Rights Council, and the mandate of the Special Rapporteur on the right to food in particular, promote accountability at the national level through communications to governments on alleged violations of the right to food, as well as through official visits of the countries, which facilitate public debate on the state of realization of the right to food.

Social movements and protection of human rights defenders

As demonstrated by the Latin America and Caribbean experience, social movements and the active participation of civil society are key to draw attention to the failure in the implementation of laws and to shed light on the situations where other accountability mechanisms fail. In recent years, civil society organizations have become more active in supervising the protection and realization of the right to food, as demonstrated by the growing number of civil society reports to support the continuous monitoring of this right at the national level.[36] In some cases, participating in campaigns to defend the right to food has important costs for the people involved, who may be subjected to physical threats and intimidation. Thus, ensuring the protection of human rights defenders is essential to guarantee accountability.

B. EFFECTIVE IMPLEMENTATION

Coordination across different sectors

It is necessary to have a multisectoral approach to promote the realization of the right to food. Guaranteeing the realization of the right to food goes beyond constitutional provisions and NFS laws, for it also depends on a series of laws and regulations related to access to land, employment, social security, safe-drinking water, etc. Therefore, a key challenge for the effective application of NFS policies and strategies is to have an effective coordination between the different sectors and ministries.

Costa Rica, Guatemala, Paraguay, Uruguay and Venezuela). The Protocol shall enter into force after its tenth ratification.

36 See for example the reports available in the website of the Observatorio de Derecho a la Alimentación de América Latina, www.oda-alc.org/front/documentos (last accessed on 10 February 2015).

All NFS laws currently in force or under consideration establish inter-sectorial bodies to coordinate the actions of the different ministries. In most cases, a National Council on NFS is created as a managing body of the system, related to the highest level of Government (Presidency or Vice-Presidency) and conformed by different ministries and civil society representatives. The state of those NFS Councils differs from one country to another. In the Brazilian case, the NFS Council (CONSEA) has a consultative character and makes recommendations to the Inter-Ministerial NFS Chamber, the working group in charge of applying the national NFS strategy,[37] despite its highly representative character. In other countries such as Guatemala, Ecuador and Nicaragua, the coordinating body can make binding decisions, but is less representative.

In some cases, the coordinating bodies have been established through an executive decree instead of a NFS law, such as the *Consejo Nacional de Alimentación y Nutrición* (CONAN) in Bolivia, the *Secretaría Nacional de Coordinación y Seguimiento del Plan Nacional* (SENAPAN) in Panama and the *Consejo Nacional de Seguridad Alimentaria y Nutricional* (CONASAN) in El Salvador.[38] These bodies have a weaker legal status than that of the institutions created by NFS laws, since executive decrees are easier to derogate than laws approved by Parliament.

These coordinating bodies generally include the ministries of agriculture, health, social affairs and education, and in some cases they have a technical secretariat located within one of such ministries. For example, in Bolivia the secretariat of CONAN is located within the Ministry of Health, while in El Salvador the Ministry of Social Inclusion coordinates the CONASAN.

Participation

Besides coordinating the application of policies and strategies by different sectors and ministries, the coordinating bodies must facilitate the participation of civil society in the formulation of policies, the identification

37 Report of the Special Rapporteur on the right to food, *Mission to Brazil*, A/HRC/13/33/Add.6 (19 February 2009), para. 14.

38 Respectively established by Executive Decree no. 27029 of 2003 (Bolivia), later modified by Decree no. 28667 (2006) to allow the participation of civil society; Decree of 18 October 2004 (Panama); and Executive Decree no. 63 of 2009 (El Salvador).

of priorities and specific measures and the follow-up through continuous consultations and dialogue, to create or expand programs that have priority to fulfill the right to food.

Ideally, NFS Councils can enable a permanent dialogue between Government and civil society organizations. The NFS Councils of Ecuador, Guatemala, Honduras and Nicaragua currently reserve seats for civil society representatives, despite its still-weak resonance in comparison to that of the representatives of Government. In this sense, the NFS Council of Brazil stands out for having a representation composed primarily by civil society (two thirds of the members).[39] Nevertheless, contrary to other NFS councils, the NFS Council of Brazil doesn't have decision-making powers. In all cases, the real decision-making power lies in the Government. For example, the NFS Council of Honduras makes simple majority decisions and is composed by twelve members, seven of which are from the Ministries of the Interior, Social Development, Agriculture, Environment, Health, Finance, and Planning and External Cooperation, while the remaining five places are reserved for civil society, representing non-governmental organizations, the National Council of private companies, the National Federation of development unions and the national organization of farmers.

There are also other mechanisms through which civil society can participate in the formulation and implementation of NFS policies. For example, in Honduras civil society participates in the local entities supervising the *Estrategia para la Reducción de la Pobreza* (Strategy for the Reduction of Poverty). In Peru, civil society is represented in the *Comisión Interministerial de Asuntos Sociales* (Inter-Ministerial Commission for Social Affairs). In Venezuela, civil society can participate through the *Asambleas Agrarias* (Agricultural Assemblies) and the *Consejos Comunales* (Communal Councils).

It's important to point out that NFS councils in Ecuador, Guatemala, Honduras and Nicaragua also allow the participation of the private sector, while other countries such as Brazil, Guatemala, Peru, Nicaragua, Panama,

---

39 Despite not being decided yet, the participation of civil society organizations is being studied by the coordinating bodies of Bolivia (Consejo Nacional de la Alimentación y Nutrición), Argentina (Comisión Nacional de Nutrición y Alimentación) and Colombia (Comité Nacional de Prevención y Control de Micronutrientes).

Venezuela, Colombia and Honduras actually promote it. The participation of private sector representatives could ideally favor a learning process for the whole food system, from the farmer to the consumer, allowing governments to identify the blockades and to improve the sustainability of the entire system.

Focus of programs

The programs to guarantee the realization of the right to food must give priority to the people and groups that are most vulnerable and that face the biggest challenges in the access to adequate food. Legal frameworks can facilitate that orientation, clearly identifying the criteria that must be met to have a right to access certain programs. All NFS laws currently in force foresee an explicit focus and prioritization of vulnerable groups. As a general tendency, food and nutrition policies and programs in the Region must give priority to children in school and pre-school ages, teenagers, pregnant and lactating women, indigenous groups and families that live in extreme poverty.

Nevertheless, the general orientation of NFS laws has to be crafted with a focus on specific programs. Besides, even though laws can usefully define the basic criteria that must guide the focus of policies and programs, ensuring that those programs reach the people with most needs can also depend upon other factors in practice. An important element is that governments must be capable of gathering sufficient information on the vulnerabilities experienced by the different communities and geographic locations, through vulnerability maps for example, based on the information obtained locally. There must also be adequate mechanisms to monitor and verify the information collected and used to identify the beneficiaries of the programs, to ensure transparency and to protect against the use of political criteria in the beneficiary selection process.

Allocation of costs and budgets

The efficient functioning of institutional frameworks and strategies for the realization of the right to food requires the allocation of sufficient resources to allow a good functioning of the national NFS systems. It is also fundamental that full transparency on the use of public resources destined for NFS programs exists, in line with the State obligation under the ICESCR and other international human rights instruments to adopt measures to the maximum of available resources for the progressive realization of the right to food.

Almost all NFS laws refer to the need to allocate sufficient resources to the policies and programs in order to ensure the progressive realization of the right to food. Nevertheless, only the NFS law of Guatemala refers to this aspect in a detailed manner. In the case of Nicaragua, the NFS law foresees the establishment of a national NFS fund, even though such fund doesn't appear to be operational yet. A similar fund established by virtue of the NFS law of 2003 in Ecuador never became operational. In the case of Guatemala, article 38 of the NFS law provides for the allocation of a minimum of 0,5 percent of the general State budget to the programs of nutritional and food safety and to projects for the population living in poverty or extreme poverty. Such funds are channeled to ministries and institutions through the *Consejo Nacional de Seguridad Alimentaria y Nutricional* (CONASAN).

Thus, the NFS law of Guatemala is the only one to ensure a minimum level of resources for the implementation of NFS programs. However, as the Attorney General for Human Rights points out in its follow-up report on the implementation of a national NFS policy, even the specific reference to a minimum amount (0,5 percent of the general budget) destined for a specific population group is not sufficiently solid to ensure its effective implementation in practice. The report also mentions the lack of an effective monitoring methodology for the budgetary allocations provided to the ministries involved in NFS programs, and highlights the problem that people are only able to reclaim their rights if the information on public spending by the Government on NFS programs is accessible to the general public.[40] As we mentioned before, the Attorney General for Human Rights also points out the issue of a high dependence on foreign aid for NFS activities, which may have negative repercussions on the allocations from the national budget with the country's own funding.

---

40 Procurador de los Derechos Humanos de Guatemala, *Primer Informe de Seguimiento a la Política Nacional de Seguridad Alimentaria y Nutricional del Gobierno de Guatemala: Resumen Ejecutivo*, 2008, pp. 63–69.

VII. LESSONS LEARNED

The experience of the countries of Latin America and the Caribbean in strengthening the institutional frameworks for the progressive realization of the right to food offers a series of lessons learned for the improvement of NFS systems.

Political will

A common experience across the region is that laws and policies by themselves do not promote the realization of the right to food, and that there is often a gap between laws and policies in writing and their implementation in practice. For laws and policies based on human rights to be implemented in practice, they must be supported by a true political will, as well as by effective monitoring and accountability mechanisms.

Adequate resources

One of the elements that define political will is the allocation of financial resources. It is necessary to include in the national budget the allocations that are necessary for the implementation of NFS policies and strategies, and to ensure their financial sustainability. An inadequate allocation of resources for the implementation of NFS laws is still a significant problem across the region, and mechanisms to ensure that the budgetary allocations correspond to the real needs are lacking.

Evaluation of needs and of results

Budgetary allocations and the focus of programs need to be based on a continuous evaluation of needs and of results of NFS programs. In particular, mechanisms must be set up to gather data on the situation and needs of vulnerable groups, including information gathered through participative processes with the communities and individuals concerned. A continuous data gathering is essential for the development of effective NFS strategies and programs, as well as to monitor their implementation in practice.

An effective coordination

Experiences in the region underline the importance and challenge of ensuring an adequate coordination among multiple actors in the implementation of NFS programs and policies. To improve and guarantee the effectiveness of the coordinating bodies that have been established, it is essential that there is an allocation of sufficient resources and powers, and that they are inclusive and open to the participation of all interested stakeholders, including civil society.

Inclusion and legitimacy of processes

A common problem in the region has been that NFS strategies and programs often don't survive Government transitions, undermining their sustainability and efficacy. Anchoring those programs in specific legislation might be useful to address this issue. It is also important for the sustainability of NFS strategies to ensure that civil society, social movements and farmers' organizations are involved in the design and execution of programs for the realization of the right to food. The pressure exercised by civil society organizations is also useful to ensure the continuity of programs and strategies.

The experience of the countries in the region underlines the importance of formulating laws and programs through inclusive and participatory processes. The wider the political participation and space given to interested stakeholders from civil society is, the more likely it will be that the law will be effective, sustainable and respected by all parties concerned.

Accountability and justiciability

Despite the progress achieved to include the right to food in national legislations, the monitoring mechanisms for the implementation of this right are still weak. More efforts are needed to empower right holders to effectively reclaim their right to food. In addition to ensuring the availability and accessibility of redress mechanisms, there must be awareness on the right to food being a prerogative guaranteed by national laws and international human rights treaties. People need to know their rights in order for them to be able to demand changes and accountability from their Government. At the same time, human rights holders and those charged with monitoring the implementation of laws and policies need to understand the obligations imposed by the right to food.

The applicability of laws related to the right to food requires something more than implementation mechanisms: it also requires a change in mentality and the creation of a culture of rights. In spite of the progress achieved, programs to fight hunger and malnutrition are still perceived as social solidarity programs instead of programs promoting human rights. In order to create a culture of rights and accountability, the information on the guarantees of specific programs and on the specific responsibilities of different actors must be readily available. Accountability mechanisms, including administrative and judicial mechanisms that allow beneficiaries to complain if their rights are arbitrarily denied, must be integrated within those programs.

It is necessary to encourage and promote that domestic courts and tribunals as well as national human rights institutions (Ombudsmen, Attorney General for Human Rights, etc.) provide reparations for violations of the right to food. Several national human rights institutions, such as those of Guatemala, El Salvador and Colombia, have begun to monitor the implementation of the right to food. National human rights institutions in the entire region should have a mandate to oversee the right to food, including through the consideration of specific cases.

The need for additional measures

Significant progress has been achieved in Latin America and the Caribbean in recent years. However, progress has been unequal and the right to adequate food is still unfulfilled for a significant proportion of the population in the region. Besides, despite the advances made in including the right to food in national legal frameworks, effective monitoring mechanisms and access to justice are still needed for the fulfillment of that right. Therefore, the progress achieved in the implementation of the right to food must be maintained and strengthened.

It is the role of government and parliaments to develop the legal frameworks to ensure progress towards the complete eradication of hunger and malnutrition and the full enjoyment of the right to adequate food. It is necessary to establish clear goals and effective mechanisms for coordination and monitoring, and to institutionalize the dialogue between Government and civil society to identify solutions and ensure accountability in the application of laws, policies and programs.

THE FUTURE IS NOW: ELIMINATING INEQUALITIES IN SANITATION, WATER, AND HYGIENE

Catarina DE ALBUQUERQUE*

I. INTRODUCTION

There is a need to redefine progress within the context of development. In the 21st century, progress must no longer continue to mask inequalities. When millions of children, women and men have no access to essential services such as sanitation or water, a global development agenda cannot continue to ignore their daily reality. The future development agenda must include measures to determine how progress is distributed and who is excluded. It must create incentives to reduce inequalities and focus on the most disadvantaged. In other words, the post-2015 development agenda must fully integrate equality and non-discrimination. We must act now as the future is now.

Growing inequalities across and within regions and countries are increasingly signaled to nuance and even challenge some of the Millennium Development Goal (MDG) achievements. There is increasing awareness of the high social cost of inequalities, resulting in disillusionment – in particular among youth –, instability and violence. Inequalities hinder efforts for poverty reduction and economic growth,[1] negatively affecting

---

* Former UN Special Rapporteur on the human right to safe-drinking water and sanitation (2008–2014). This article was originally written for the post-2015 thematic consultation on water in 2013. I want to thank OHCHR staff as well as Dr. Inga Winkler, Ms. Virginia Roaf and Ms. Johanna Gusman for their support with preparing this paper.

1 C. MELAMED, *Putting inequality in the post-2015 picture*, Overseas Development Institute (ODI), London 2012, p. 4.

society as a whole.[2] In fact, the World Economic Forum cited inequality as one of the top global risks.[3] For major international actors and agencies, including the United Nations Children's Fund (UNICEF) and UN-Women, addressing inequalities is vital to their work. There is also a shared understanding in the water and sanitation sectors that the MDGs did not put sufficient pressure on Governments to ensure their efforts are reaching the poorest and most marginalized populations.[4]

Inequalities are present in every country across the globe, yet, they manifest themselves differently across regions and within countries. Some types of discrimination such as that based on gender, age or disability status are relevant in all countries, while others – such as ethnic discrimination – can take diverse shapes from country to country. Despite these country differences, inequalities and disparities are structural factors. While the specific groups may vary, patterns of marginalization, exclusion and discrimination are consistent across the world. Showing these patterns and trends through global monitoring conveys a powerful message and provides a tool to draw attention to the situation of the most disadvantaged and marginalized. In turn, global monitoring assists Governments to develop the necessary laws, policies and programmes that will lead to elimination of the gap between those groups and individuals with access and those without it.

The last decade has seen a significant evolution in the human rights framework, enhancing the tools to address growing concerns about inequality in the enjoyment of economic, social and cultural rights. While the rights to water and sanitation have always been a component of the right to an adequate standard of living as contained in several international human rights instruments, their explicit recognition by the UN General Assembly and the Human Rights Council in 2010[5] created enormous

2 UN Task Team on the Post-2015 UN Development Agenda, *Addressing inequalities: The heart of the post-2015 agenda and the future we want for all*, United Nations, 2012, p. 6.

3 World Economic Forum, *Global Risks Report 2012*, 7th ed., WEF, Geneva 2012, p. 19.

4 World Health Organization (WHO) and United Nations Children's Fund (UNICEF) Joint Monitoring Programme, *Report of the first Consultation on Post-2015 Monitoring of Drinking-water and Sanitation*, WHO/UNICEF, Berlin 2011.

5 General Assembly, *The human right to water and sanitation*, A/RES/64/292 (03 August 2010); Human Rights Council, *Human rights and access to safe drinking water and sanitation*, A/HRC/RES/15/9 (6 October 2010).

momentum in the sector, galvanizing international support to increase resources and scale up efforts to ensure access to water and sanitation for all. More generally, a deeper understanding of economic, social and cultural rights in the last decade,[6] coupled with further guidance about the effects of non-discrimination in the realization of these rights[7] has allowed for the development of a more discernible human rights framework around these issues. These evolutions must permeate the post-2015 global development agenda.

Every country in the world has committed to realizing human rights, including the human rights to water and sanitation. The post-2015 agenda must be universal in scope so as to reflect this commitment, and ambitious enough to respond to the reality of daily lives. The focus on achieving equality is relevant for every country, including developed countries where a relatively small number of people are left without (adequate) access to services, and aggregate targets may not reflect the effort required to reach these individuals and households. The new framework must ensure that Governments prioritize the populations most in need.

For the next set of goals, it is not acceptable to disregard acute development challenges – as inequalities – simply because they do not fit into certain definable categories or because we have difficulties in measuring them. It is also not acceptable to reshape or limit them to fit with the comfortable limits of current knowledge. While many caution that future targets and indicators need to be measurable, and this is certainly true, there is also a tendency to hide behind this technical argument. Others have noted that measurability is an inappropriate standard for political decisions and that data should "be seen as a servant, rather than a master".[8] The future framework must measure what is valuable and not value only what is

6 This deeper understanding was also facilitated by the adoption of the Optional Protocol to the International Covenant on Economic, Social and Cultural Rights which gave the opportunity to address misconceptions about economic, social and cultural rights at international and national levels, including in relation to monitoring, accountability and access to remedies.

7 UN Committee on Economic, Social and Cultural Rights, *General Comment No. 20: Non-discrimination in economic, social and cultural rights*, E/C.12/GC/20 (2 July 2009).

8 UN Task Team on the Post-2015 UN Development Agenda, *Addressing inequalities: The heart of the post-2015 agenda and the future we want for all*, United Nations, 2012, p. 13.

measurable. Therefore, data must be collected on issues such as inequalities precisely to bring them to light. The current lack of data may not be accidental: neglect often coincides with a low political profile. One example of this, present in many countries, is that of people living in informal settlements who do not appear in official statistics. The boundaries of what is currently perceived as measurable must be pushed. A commitment to better and more accurate data collection is essential to identify and monitor inequalities, a crucial step to making progress to end them.

II. EMBRACING NON-DISCRIMINATION, EQUALITY AND EQUITY

Non-discrimination and equality are fundamental human rights principles; development actors often use the notion of equity. These concepts must be understood before their integration into goals, targets and indicators is discussed.

- **Non-discrimination** is one of the pillars of international human rights law. Discrimination is defined as any distinction, exclusion or restriction which has the purpose or the effect of impairing or nullifying the recognition, enjoyment or exercise, on an equal basis with others, of human rights and fundamental freedoms in the political, economic, social, cultural, civil or any other field.[9] In terms of monitoring, this principle requires States to look beyond average attainments and disaggregate data sets in order to identify disparate impacts or less favorable treatment over time.

- **Equality before the law and equal protection of the law** without any discrimination, constitute basic principles relating to the protection and enjoyment of human rights. They require a focus on all groups and individuals experiencing discrimination. Substantive equality calls for adoption of affirmative action or temporary special measures where barriers exist and persist, and which lead to denial of rights to individuals and groups.

---

9 See for example Article 1.1 of the Convention on the Elimination of Racial Discrimination; Article 1 of the Convention on the Elimination of all Forms of Discrimination against Women; or Article 2 of the Convention of the Rights of Persons with Disabilities.

Equal, however, does not mean the same. Equality does not imply treating what is unequal equally. Under human rights law, there is a necessary distinction, as equality does not indicate identical treatment in all cases. While universality is about ensuring access for all – even the hardest to reach – equality is about "leveling up" or progressively working to improve the quality and levels of service for groups that lag behind. In relation to water, sanitation and hygiene, equality presumes, for example, gradual improvements to close gaps in unequal coverage rates. Human rights law requires equal access to basic services, but this does not mean that everyone benefits from the same technical solutions or the same type of service.

- **Equity** is the moral imperative to dismantle unjust differences based on principles of fairness and justice. It requires a focus on the most disadvantaged and the poorest. Many organizations in the sector, including the Water Supply and Sanitation Collaborative Council, WaterAid, the World Health Organization and the UNICEF, have made equity a central part of their agenda. However, from a human rights perspective, relying on equity has certain risks because its definition is a malleable concept that is not legally binding. While equity may denote justice, it may dilute rights claims if considered separately from equality and non-discrimination and risks being defined arbitrarily according to political and ideological expedience.

Embracing the human rights principles of non-discrimination and equality, combined with the equity approach must be central to any post-2015 framework. They provide the necessary political foundation to identify and prioritize a State's legal obligation to combat discrimination while also underscoring areas where human rights law has been traditionally less robust, particularly in relation to income disparities.

III. REMEDYING INEQUALITY AS THE MOST SIGNIFICANT BLIND-SPOT IN THE MILLENIUM DEVELOPMENT GOALS

The MDGs are silent on discrimination, inequalities and unjustifiable disparities. In theory, many of the targets could be achieved without benefitting a single person with a disability, a single person belonging to an ethnic minority, or a single person living in poverty, because their focus on average attainments creates a blind-spot in the achievement of equality.

UNICEF has taken a lead role by placing equity at the centre of its development agenda, recognizing that reaching the poorest and most marginalized communities within countries is pivotal to the realization of the Goals.[10] Likewise, UN-Women has also cautioned that, with the target date of 2015 in sight, it is increasingly clear that progress towards meeting many of the Goals, particularly those strongly related to gender inequality, is off-track. Inequality, including gender inequality, is holding back progress.[11] The United Nations System Task Team on the Post-2015 Development Agenda put forward equality as one of the fundamental principles providing the foundation for the post-2015 agenda alongside human rights and sustainability.[12] Unless action is taken to address discrimination and inequalities, the post-2015 goals will fail to address the underlying truth behind the figures: MDG indicators are consistently worse for discriminated groups in every region.[13]

In many countries, specific groups are excluded from access to water and sanitation often reflecting patterns of discrimination and marginalization. These groups can be identified along ethnic and socio-economic divides.[14] In some countries, indigenous peoples do not have access to water or sanitation services.[15] Dalits often suffer discrimination in accessing water and sanitation,[16] while Roma are marginalized with respect to water and

---

10 UNICEF, *Progress for Children: Achieving the MDGs with equity*, UNICEF, New York 2010, p. 6.

11 UN Women, *Progress of the World's Women: Gender Justice and the Millennium Development Goals*, UN Women, New York 2011, available at http://progress.unwomen.org/pdfs/EN-Report-Progress.pdf (last accessed on 20 February 2015).

12 *Id.*, p. 116.

13 C. MELAMED, above n 1, at 4.

14 Report of the Special Rapporteur on the human right to safe drinking water and sanitation, *Mission to the United States of America*, A/HRC/18/33/Add.4 (2 August 2011), par. 79.

15 Report of the Special Rapporteur on the human right to safe drinking water and sanitation, *Mission to Costa* Rica, A/HRC/12/24/Add.1 (23 June 2009), par. 48.

16 Report of the Special Rapporteur on the human right to safe drinking water and sanitation, *Mission to Bangladesh*, A/HRC/15/55 (22 July 2010), par. 25.

sanitation in many European countries.[17] Moreover, there are vast gender inequalities – women and girls are overwhelmingly tasked with collecting water.[18] Persons with disabilities are also disproportionately represented among those who lack access to safe drinking water and sanitation.[19] Multiple discrimination, or the compounded impact of various grounds of discrimination, heightens the marginalization and discrimination experienced by an individual or group.

Discrimination and marginalization relate to different factors such as ethnicity, language, religion, caste, gender, age, disability, nationality, and others. While the focus of the equity discourse is often on people living in poverty, it must not be forgotten that the world's poorest are not randomly distributed – they disproportionately share one or several of the factors that commonly lead to exclusion and discrimination. In order to assess progress properly in reducing inequalities, monitoring must go beyond inequities in income because focusing on income disparities does not address the root causes of exclusion and lack of access to social development. Examining these other factors explains why people lack access and helps to design appropriate policy responses. A person with a disability and a person of an ethnic minority might be both poor and lacking access to water and/ or sanitation – but the reasons for their lack of access differ, and the necessary policy response to guarantee them access are also distinct. Sometimes, the barrier preventing certain individuals and groups from having access is not a lack of financial resources, but rather the existence of discriminatory laws, policies, cumbersome administrative procedures, stereotypes, or unequal power relations that lead to their exclusion. Moreover, without targeting the most marginalized, they will continue to be excluded even when efforts target the poorest of the poor.

---

17 Report of the Special Rapporteur on the human right to safe drinking water and sanitation, *Mission to Slovenia*, A/HRC/18/33/Add.2 (3 September 2010), par. 33.

18 Report of the Special Rapporteur on the human right to safe drinking water and sanitation, *Mission to Egypt*, A/HRC/15/31/Add.3 (5 July 2010), par. 22.

19 Report of the Special Rapporteur on the human right to safe drinking water and sanitation, *Mission to Bangladesh*, A/HRC/15/55 (22 July 2010), par. 21.

IV. INTEGRATING EQUALITY AND NON-DISCRIMINATION INTO THE FUTURE FRAMEWORK: A STAND-ALONE GOAL ON EQUALITY

The post-2015 development agenda must be ambitious and forward-looking. It must tackle disparities and identify non-discrimination and equality as core principles. Appallingly, much of the progress made since 2000 has left the most marginalized individuals and groups in the same situation they were in when the MDGs were designed. Indeed, many agree that the current set of MDGs, which focus on average global progress, has masked the inequalities that lie behind these averages. This sentiment is widely shared by those working in the water and sanitation sectors, commenting that, "concerns of non-discrimination and equity related to fulfilling the right to access water and sanitation should be reflected in future indicators."[20] For the future framework, better tools and methodologies for measuring the underlying inequalities need to be developed.

Already in 2010, States committed to improved systems for monitoring progress towards the MDGs, so as to allow for the collection of disaggregated data to capture inequalities by recognizing that, "all countries require adequate, timely, reliable and disaggregated data, including demographic data, in order to design better programmes and policies for sustainable development".[21]The MDG framework calls for disaggregation of data according to different stratifiers such as sex to the greatest extent possible.[22] Experience has shown, though, that such calls are not sufficient in themselves – they need to be linked to goals and targets that offer an incentive for progress in reducing inequalities. Data constraints often reflect a lack of political commitment – they must no longer be used as an excuse to mask inequalities.

20 World Health Organization (WHO) and United Nations Children's Fund (UNICEF) Joint Monitoring Programme (JMP), *Report of the first Consultation on Post-2015 Monitoring of Drinking-water and Sanitation*, WHO/UNICEF, Berlin 2011, p. 3.

21 General Assembly, *Keeping the promise: united to achieve the Millennium Development Goals*, A/RES/65/1 (19 October 2010), par. 68.

22 United Nations Statistics Division, *Official List of Millennium Development Goal Indicators*, 2008, available at http://mdgs.un.org/unsd/mdg/Host.aspx?Content=indicators/officiallist.htm (last accessed on 20 February 2015).

By itself, disaggregation of data does not automatically result in the reduction of inequalities. It provides a tool for the collection of more detailed and accurate data, but policy-makers need to act on the information it reveals. The real challenge lies at the political level because the way in which development, poverty and their inherent inequalities are measured has tremendous influence on the direction of policies, the allocation of resources and the effectiveness of responses. Therefore, the aim of reducing inequalities must not only be captured at the level of disaggregation of indicators, but must be reflected in specific goals and targets against which progress can be measured.

The post-2015 framework must be designed explicitly to reveal who remains invisible and where past efforts have been insufficient. Based on these findings, goals and targets must be framed in a way to reduce inequalities and target the most disadvantaged. They must not continue to focus solely on aggregate outcomes. This process' inherent difficulty should not detract from the fact that it is a legal and moral imperative. Inclusion of goals and targets that focus on eliminating inequalities within the post-2015 framework will help draw attention to the groups and individuals most in need, trigger the creation of more precise data and adjust development aims and policies to better respond to the reality on the ground.

In response to concerns about inequalities in progress, some have proposed that future targets be made universal, so that no group can be left behind.[23] The goal could not be considered achieved unless everyone is reached. However, setting universal access as the goal – as laudable and necessary as it is – is insufficient to ensure priority for the most disadvantaged groups and individuals. Universal access at a specified target date would continue to bring focus on aggregate outcomes without setting incentives to reduce inequalities through targeting those individuals and groups that are most disadvantaged. On the contrary, specifying that a goal be "universal" alone may be an incentive for States to continue to prioritize relatively well-off and easy-to-reach individuals and groups without access, in order to demonstrate rapid progress towards the goal of universal access. Under that scenario, the most disadvantaged will often be the last to be reached.[24]

23 J. MCARTHUR, *Getting to Zero: finishing the Job the Millennium Development Goals Started*, Global Agenda Council on Benchmarking Progress, 2012.

24 UN Task Team on the Post-2015 UN Development Agenda, *Addressing inequalities: The heart of the post-2015 agenda and the future we want for all*, United Nations, 2012, p.12.

The future goals and targets must therefore explicitly embrace equality alongside universality.

Equality is relevant to all fields of development and must be applied to all future goals. To underscore the intrinsic value of equality as an overriding objective, it should also be a stand-alone goal.[25] Having a stand-alone goal on the reduction of inequality is essential to bring it to centre stage of the development agenda. While some argue that a separate equality goal will lead to an insular treatment of equality,[26] the opposite is likely to be the case: including equality as an overarching, cross-cutting concern at the goal level will ensure that the elimination of inequalities will be addressed under all the substantive targets.

Among the ideas for a dedicated goal on equality, one of the most cited proposals is to have a target for income inequality by using the Gini coefficient.[27] A target could either relate to a specific level of income equality or it could call for a reduction in the Gini coefficient until it fell below a certain value.[28] However, income inequality is not always the best proxy for measuring overall inequality. Other metrics of inequality may better capture discrimination and inequalities. Future targets should reflect the reality that poverty is often the result of multiple, intersecting forms of discrimination.

In fact, the current MDG on gender equality already represents an attempt at formulating a stand-alone goal on one particular area of equality. The accompanying target has been heavily criticized for limiting gender equality to education, which is again somewhat broadened by the indicators that also measure the share of women in wage employment and the proportion of seats in national parliament.[29] Still, the gaps between the goal and its accompanying targets and indicators related to the overall measure of

---

25 Committee for Development Policy, *The United Nations Development Strategy Beyond 2015*, United Nations, New York 2012, p. 18.

26 J. VANDEMOORTELE, *Advancing the global development agenda post-2015: some thoughts, ideas and practical suggestions*, United Nations, New York 2012, p. 21.

27 A country's Gini coefficient is between 0 and 100, with 0 indicating perfect income equality and 100 indicating absolute income inequality, meaning a single person would have all the income.

28 C. MELAMED, above n 1, p. 4.

29 Office of the UN High Commissioner for Human Rights, *Claiming the Millennium Development Goals: a human rights approach*, United Nations, Geneva 2008, p. 26.

gender equality highlight the difficulty of reducing a goal on equality to a limited number of quantifiers that can capture the different forms and manifestations of inequalities in any meaningful and comprehensive way.

The challenge is to set an overall goal on equality that does justice to its cross-cutting nature, relevance to all fields of development and different grounds and manifestations of inequalities. To address these challenges, the future development agenda could include an overall goal on achieving equality accompanied by targets for different sectors for reducing inequalities. Since it might not be necessary, feasible or advisable to relate all targets to all different grounds of discrimination, the pertaining indicators could focus on the dominant inequalities as relevant for different sectors relating to sex, disability, age, income/wealth, ethnicity, and geographic location, among other stratifiers.[30] The overall framework would have to ensure that all different types of inequalities are captured. Optionally, if indicators with ordinal values were selected, the different sectorial indicators could be combined for a composite score that would yield an overall measure of equality.

V. CRAFTING TARGETS TO ENSURE EQUAL WATER, SANITATION AND HYGIENE FOR ALL

Turning to water, sanitation and hygiene specifically, one of the challenges will be to improve the analysis of different forms of discrimination and design an appropriate methodology to monitor them. The following section highlights some manifestations of discrimination derived from international human rights law, as well as general considerations of equity. These issues could also be applied outside the water, sanitation and hygiene sector. Based on these considerations, this section also puts forward some ideas of how to integrate these into the future development goals, targets and indicators framework.

To allow for such monitoring, the data sets that are presently used include a wide variety of equity and equality-related variables which are amenable to much more equality analysis than has been performed to date. Other data

30 C. MELAMED, above n 1, p. 5.

could be generated relatively easily with slight adaptations of the current data sources and the addition of other sources to complement existing household surveys. Ongoing discussions at the technical level show that these proposals are feasible and that better monitoring of the equality dimension of access to water and sanitation can be achieved, given the required political will.[31]

A. MOVE FORWARD WHILE REDUCING INEQUALITIES

Human rights law requires States to prioritize basic access for everyone. This must be reflected in future goals, targets and indicators. Progressive realization means that expeditious and effective steps must be taken and that it is not acceptable for States to aim for universal access at the most basic level only. Instead, continual improvement toward an adequate standard of living must be the aim. However, prioritizing those lacking services and ensuring progressive realization does not by itself address non-discrimination.

Among those who are disadvantaged in their access to water and sanitation, there are many who are discriminated against – because they have a disability, because they are girls, because of where they live, or a combination of these and other factors. If these additional dimensions are not captured, the people who are discriminated against will continue to be discriminated against, even among the most disadvantaged in their access to water and sanitation.

B. ADDRESS GEOGRAPHICAL INEQUALITIES: RURAL/URBAN DISPARITIES AND SLUMS

One of the most pervasive inequities in water and sanitation exists between the urban and rural populations. Global monitoring shows that rural populations persistently have lower levels of access than urban

---

31 World Health Organization (WHO) and United Nations Children's Fund (UNICEF) Joint Monitoring Programme (JMP), *Report of the first Consultation on Post-2015 Monitoring of Drinking-water and Sanitation*, WHO/UNICEF, Berlin 2011.

populations. Geographically removed, remote and marginalized regions are often overlooked in planning. The disaggregation between rural and urban as called for in the current monitoring framework should therefore be retained, while improving the methodology to capture the situations of people living in slums.

People living in slums frequently lack access to adequate water and sanitation. Worldwide, it is estimated that a billion people live in slums, which is about one third of the urban population.[32] There are many causes for their lack of access to services, including deliberate exclusion in laws and policies of informal settlements from formal water and sanitation services.

Identifying and defining slums can pose a challenge for monitoring, but significant advances have been made in recent years, including by groups working with slum-dweller organizations and through spatial analysis. Assessing slums by their location could both yield more accurate data and serve as an effective link to planning. In addition, the definition of slums needs improvement; the best approach may be to use definitions supplied by the countries themselves. Household surveys could be complemented special slum surveys or could include oversampling in slum areas.

C. SHED LIGHT ON THE POOREST OF THE POOR

Wealth inequity correlates in many countries to inequalities in access to adequate water and sanitation. The rate of progress is very uneven among wealth quintiles in many countries, with the poorest two quintiles frequently experiencing lack of improvement while other quintiles experience significant improvements. In other countries, progress has been impressive among the lower quintiles, and lessons could be drawn from these experiences. Some Governments are reacting to this analysis by reassessing their policies and programming to target resources on those living in poverty.[33]

---

32 WHO and UN-HABITAT, *Hidden Cities: unmasking and overcoming health inequities in urban settings*, WHO/United Nations, Geneva 2010.

33 For more details, see JMP Working Group on Equity and Non-Discrimination, *Final Report*, Lisbon 2012, available at www.wssinfo.org/fileadmin/user_upload/resources/JMP-END-WG-Final-Report-20120821.pdf (last accessed on 20 February 2015).

The wealth-quintile analysis is very powerful in highlighting the inequities in access to water and sanitation, and also in showing that States are in a position to improve this situation with the necessary political will. The new framework should reflect the need for this analysis at the level of targets. Hence targets should be crafted that specifically address improvements for the lowest quintile or call for eliminating the inequalities between the best-off and the worst-off.

D. ADDRESS GROUP-RELATED INEQUALITIES THAT VARY ACROSS COUNTRIES

The impacts of discrimination on access to water, sanitation and hygiene are often due to income disparities, but often they go beyond lack of resources. The dynamics and systems involved in discrimination against minorities and the impacts of wealth inequities are different. Data can assist in elucidating these differences, helping to catalyze action in relation to the specific problems present in a given context.

Pilot analysis carried in the framework of the Working Group on Equity and Non-discrimination of the WHO/UNICEF Joint Monitoring Programme for Water Supply and Sanitation demonstrated that significant disparities exist in water and sanitation access among ethnic, religious, and language minorities in some countries. For example in one South Asian country, data show that while open defecation rates for the majority population was 37%, the rate for the minority population was 70%. A rights-sensitive analysis uncovers such patterns so that factors leading to these differences can be explored and policy responses be developed. If the progress of groups that suffer discrimination and marginalization is not specifically monitored, those groups will remain excluded – even among the poorest.

Targets and indicators should therefore specifically address the "most disadvantaged groups". As discrimination manifests itself differently across regions and within countries and groups discriminated against vary by country, the formulation "most disadvantaged groups" is recommended, allowing for national specificity while making global monitoring possible. States would be required to identify the specific groups that will be monitored at the global level through a participatory process.[34] Groups that might be chosen for monitoring include those defined by ethnicity, race, religion, language, or spatially defined groups such as slum-dwellers, residents of specific geographic areas, or other nationally tailored groupings.

E. ADDRESS INEQUALITIES DUE TO INDIVIDUAL STATUS RELEVANT IN EVERY COUNTRY

Evidence shows that women and girls, older people, persons living with chronic diseases or with disabilities often face particular barriers in accessing water and sanitation, and that these barriers are experienced both within the household and when accessing community and public facilities. Global monitoring data have demonstrated that women and girls shoulder the burden of collecting household water, which restricts their time for other activities, including education, work and rest. Moreover, when households share sanitation facilities, women and girls may be required by social norms on privacy to avoid using the facilities except during hours of darkness, when their personal safety may be at increased risk. When sanitation and water facilities are not designed with them in mind, older persons and those with physical access constraints, including disabilities, may face obstacles to using these facilities. Such discrimination based on sex/gender, age, disability, and health status occurs across the globe and in all strata of society.

Human rights law requires that effective measures be taken to end discriminatory impacts based on sex/gender, disability, age, and health status in all fields and to eliminate inequalities wherever they occur. States are obliged to take measures to enhance equality in all places, both public and private spheres. While human rights law does not require Governments to provide water directly or to build sanitation facilities wherever they are lacking, it does oblige Governments to take steps to ensure that everyone can access these rights without discrimination. In government-run institutions such as primary schools, hospitals, or places of detention, direct provision of services is required.

34 World Health Organization (WHO) and United Nations Children's Fund (UNICEF) Joint Monitoring Programme (JMP), *Report of the first Consultation on Post-2015 Monitoring of Drinking-water and Sanitation*, WHO/UNICEF, Berlin 2011, p. 3.

Much has been learned through questions in household surveys about intra-household inequalities related to water collection. Much less is known about inequalities concerning access to, and use of, sanitation and hygiene, and about intra-household inequalities concerning age and disability. Given that not all households share resources and assets equally among their members and that some may be relatively more privileged than others, it is imperative to accurately disaggregate intra-household data. There is evidence that intra-household inequality and poverty may disproportionately affect women, persons with disabilities, children and older persons. Targets and indicators should be phrased in a way that requires monitoring of intra-household inequalities. This would shine a powerful light on areas that need change, but remain often invisible.

In addition, it would be valuable to monitor how gender, age, and disability-related inequalities manifest themselves in relation to water, sanitation, and hygiene in public facilities such as schools, health facilities, work places, prisons and other detention centers. Indeed, such inequalities may be even more acute in public spaces, making the collection of data about equality variables especially important.

One particular area where individual inequalities and the lack of attention to women's and girl's needs is starkly apparent is menstrual hygiene management. Menstruation is a taboo topic. Women and girls are obliged to hide their menstrual hygiene practices, limit their movements during menstruation and behave furtively. Girls may be taken out of school or workplaces or choose not to attend because there are no facilities for hygienically managing menstruation in sanitation facilities (where they exist).[35]

Because menstrual hygiene management has such a strong impact on gender equality, it could be used as a proxy for information about discrimination against women and girls in sanitation and hygiene. Targets and indicators should be crafted to capture the ability of all women and adolescent girls to manage menstruation hygienically and with dignity.

---

35 For further discussion, see A. PATKAR, *Menstrual Hygiene Management: Contributions to JMP Working Group on Equity and Non-Discrimination*, 2011, available at www.wssinfo.org/fileadmin/user_upload/resources/MENSTRUAL-HYGIENE-MANAGEMENT-Paper-for-END-group-1.pdf (last accessed on 20 February 2015).

VI. CONCLUSION

Future goals must aim at universal access to water, sanitation and hygiene, while explicitly embracing equality. Aiming at universal access alone would continue to highlight aggregate outcomes without setting incentives to put an end to inequalities. The situation of the most disadvantaged groups would continue to be hidden and neglected. To underscore the intrinsic value of equality as an overriding objective and ensure that the elimination of inequalities will be addressed under all the substantive targets, equality should be a stand-alone goal in the future framework.

Current limitations in measurements or data collection should not deter the international community from committing to a robust set of goals and targets. The boundaries of what is currently perceived as measurable must be pushed precisely to shed light on persistent inequalities.

The future framework should not stop at monitoring income disparities and general notions of inequities, but must seek to detect different types and manifestations of discrimination in order to examine and address the root causes of exclusion. It must aim to ensure social development for all, and at offering strong incentives for effective policy responses at the national level without further delay.

The future agenda must target individuals and groups defined by ethnicity, race, religion, language, caste and other stratifiers or spatially defined groups such as slum-dwellers who often experience discrimination. While the specific groups may vary, patterns of marginalization, exclusion and discrimination are consistent across the world. The groups should therefore be defined through a participatory process at the national level while also enabling global monitoring, which will bring to light their specific situation and serve to effectively ensuring that progress includes them.

The future framework must also address inequalities linked to a person's individual status such as gender, age, disability or health conditions, including in the area of menstrual hygiene management where gender inequalities and a lack of attention to women's and girl's needs is starkly apparent.

To tackle these challenges the future development framework must redefine progress and explicitly include equality, non-discrimination and equity at its foundations. It must set incentives to eliminate inequalities through focusing on the most disadvantaged and measure progress against these targets. Discrimination and inequalities have been, and still are, persistent across the globe: the new agenda must ensure that they become issues of the past.

MOVING THE HUMAN RIGHTS AND ENVIRONMENT AGENDA FORWARD

The Establishment of the Mandate on Human Rights and the Environment

John H. Knox*

I. INTRODUCTION

On 22 March 2012, the United Nations Human Rights Council (HRC) decided to appoint an Independent Expert on the issue of human rights obligations relating to the enjoyment of a safe, clean, healthy and sustainable environment.[1]

Building on several other resolutions related to human rights and the environment, the HRC requests the Independent Expert to, among other things: study the human rights obligations relating to the enjoyment of a safe, clean, healthy and sustainable environment, in consultation with relevant stakeholders; identify and promote best practices on the use of human rights obligations and commitments to inform, support and strengthen environmental policy making and prepare a compendium of best practices; and make recommendations that could help the realization of the Millennium Development Goals, in particular Goal 7; and contribute a human rights perspective to the Rio +20 follow-up process.

This short background paper presents an overview of the historical and legal context surrounding the establishment of the human rights and environment mandate. It begins by providing a short summary of how the

* UN Special Rapporteur (former Independent Expert) on Human Rights and the Environment, and Henry C. Lauerman Professor of International Law at Wake Forest University School of Law.

1 Human Rights Council, *Human rights and the environment*, A/HRC/RES/19/10 (19 April 2012).

relation between human rights and the environment has been developed in international, regional, and national contexts. Next, it summarises the major developments in the United Nations human rights system leading up to the establishment of the mandate. Finally, the paper concludes by reviewing key elements of the Independent Expert's preliminary report submitted to the 22nd Session of the Human Rights Council.

II. THE RELATION BETWEEN HUMAN RIGHTS AND ENVIRONMENT

The link between human rights and the environment has generally taken two courses: 1) linking the environment to a spectrum of substantive and procedural human rights, such as the right to life or the right to effective public participation, and 2) the establishment of a right to environment, with any number of qualifying terms, including healthy, clean, sustainable and safe. Each is briefly discussed in turn.

A. LINKING THE ENVIRONMENT TO EXISTING HUMAN RIGHTS

It is well established and understood that the state of the environment is a precondition to the full enjoyment of a wide range of human rights, including the right to life itself.[2] Indeed, the 1972 Declaration of the United Nations Conference on the Human Environment (Stockholm Declaration) emphasized this link by affirming that "both aspects of man's environment, the natural and the man-made, are essential to his

---

2 See e.g. J.H. KNOX, 'Climate Change and Human Rights Law' (2010) 50 *Va. J. Int'l L. (Virginia Journal of International Law)* 163; D. SHELTON, 'Human Rights and the Environment: Problems and Possibilities' (2008) 38:1–2 *Environmental Policy and Law* 41; L. COLLINS, 'Are We There Yet? The Right to Environment in International and European Law' (2007) 3 *McGill Int'l J. Sust. Dev. L. & Pol'y* (*McGill International Journal of Sustainable Development Law & Policy*) 119; S. ATAPATTU, 'The Right to Healthy Life or the Right to Die Polluted?: The Emergence of a Human Right to a Healthy Environment Under International Law' (2002–2003) 16 *Tul. Envtl. L. J.* (*Tulane Environmental Law Journal*) 65, 69; M.R. ANDERSON, 'Human Rights Approaches to Environmental Protection: An Overview' in A. BOYLE and M. ANDERSON (eds.), *Human Rights Approaches to Environmental Protection*, Oxford University Press, Oxford 1996.

well-being and to the enjoyment of basic human rights – even the right to life itself." Principle 1 of the Declaration further stated that "Man has the fundamental right to freedom, equality and adequate conditions of life, in an environment of a quality that permits a life of dignity and well-being, and he bears solemn responsibility to protect and improve the environment for present and future generations."

The Office of the High Commissioner for Human Rights (OHCHR) discussed these links in its study on the relationship between climate change and the enjoyment of a range of human rights, including the right to life, the right to adequate food, the right to water, the right to health, and the right to adequate housing.[3] For example, the report linked the projected effects of climate change, such as heat waves, floods, storms, fires and droughts, to an increase in deaths, disease, and injury.[4] With respect to the right to adequate housing, the report explained that sea level rise and storm surges will have a direct impact on many coastal settlements and that informal settlements – often built in hazardous areas such as riverbanks and fragile hillsides – will be particularly vulnerable to extreme climate events.[5]

The link between human rights and the environment has also been addressed by a wide array of international and regional instruments and mechanisms, including human rights treaty bodies, United Nations resolutions[6] and Special Procedures, and multi-lateral environmental agreements. For instance, the Committee on Economic, Social, and Cultural Rights explains that article 12 of the Convention on Economic, Social and Cultural Rights – which provides for the right to health – "embraces a wide range of socio-economic factors that promote conditions in which people can lead a healthy life, and extends to the underlying determinants of health, such as food and nutrition, housing, access to safe and potable water and adequate sanitation, safe and healthy working conditions, and a healthy environment".

---

3 *Report of the Office of the United Nations High Commissioner for Human rights on the relationship between climate change and human rights*, A/HRC/10/61 (15 January 2009).

4 *Id.*, para. 22.

5 *Id.*, para. 37.

6 A series of Human Rights Council and General Assembly Resolutions explicitly linking human rights with the environment are discussed in section III.

Moreover, regional human rights tribunals have played a significant role in clarifying the relationship between various human rights obligations and the environment, including decisions holding that environmental harm has resulted in violations of the rights to life[7], health[8], property[9], and privacy.[10] For additional discussion of international law developments linking the environment to substantive human rights, readers are referred to further literature on this topic.[11]

In addition to linking the environment to substantive human rights, there is wide consensus that the fulfilment of certain procedural human rights are necessary to protect the environment, namely the human rights of access to information, public participation, freedom of expression and association, and access to justice.[12] The rationale is that the exercise

---

7 See e.g. African Commission on Human and Peoples' Rights, communication No. 155/96, *Social and Economic Rights Action Center* v. *Nigeria (Ogoniland Case)*, decision, para. 67; European Court of Human Rights, *Öneryildiz* v. *Turkey* (application No. 48939/99), Judgement, 30 November 2004, para. 118; Inter-American Commission on Human Rights, *Report on the situation of human rights in Ecuador*, document OEA/Ser.L/V/II.96 doc. 10 rev. 1.

8 See e.g., European Committee of Social Rights, complaint No. 30/2005, *Marangopoulos Foundation for Human Rights* v. *Greece*, para. 221.

9 See e.g. Inter-American Court of Human Rights, *Saramaka People* v. *Suriname*, Series C No. 172, judgement of 28 November 2007, paras. 95, 158; *Indigenous Community of Yakye Axa* v. *Paraguay*, Series C No. 125, judgement of 17 June 2005, para. 143, 156; Inter-American Commission on Human Rights, *Maya Indigenous Community of the Toledo District* v. *Belize*, case 12.053, report No. 40/04, document OEA/Ser.L/V/II.122, doc. 5 rev. 1, para. 153.

10 See e.g., European Court of Human Rights, *Fadeyeva v. Russia* (application No. 55723/00), judgement of 9 June 2005, para. 134; *Taşkin and others* v. *Turkey* (application No. 46117/99), judgement of 10 November 2004, para. 126; *López Ostra* v. *Spain* (application No. 16798/90), judgement of 9 December 1994, para. 58.

11 See e.g. L. COLLINS, above n 2; S. ATAPATTU, above n 2; J. KNOX, above n 2; D. SHELTON, above n 2.

12 See e.g. S. ATAPATTU, above n 2; A. BOYLE, 'Human Rights or Environmental Rights? A Reassessment' (2006–2007) 18 *Fordham Envtl. L. Rev.* (*Fordham Environmental Law Review*) 471; OHCHR and UNEP, *Human Rights and the Environment. Rio+20: Joint Report*, United Nations, 2012; Report of the Special Rapporteur on the adverse effects of the illicit movement and dumping of toxic and dangerous products and wastes, *Human rights and the environment*, E/CN.4/Sub.2/1994/9 (6 July 1994), and its Annex I, *Draft Principles on Human Rights and the Environment*; D. SHELTON, above n 2; R. PICOLOTTI, 'Agenda 21 and Human Rights: The Right to Partcipate' in R. PICOLOTTI and J.D. TAILLANT (eds.), *Linking Human Rights and the Environment*, University of Arizona Press, Tucson

of such rights results in policies and decisions that better reflect the concerns of individuals and communities who are potentially impacted by environmental harm.[13]

These procedural rights are well-recognised in an array of international human rights instruments. Although they do not specifically elaborate these rights within the context of environmental protection, they clearly apply in such circumstances.[14]

For example, with respect to the right of access to information, article 19 of the Universal Declaration of Human Rights provides that "Everyone has the right to freedom of opinion and expression; this right includes freedom to hold opinions without interference and to seek, receive and impart information and ideas through any media and regardless of frontiers." Moreover, article 19.2 of the International Covenant on Civil and Political Rights (ICCPR) states that "Everyone shall have the right to freedom of expression; this right shall include freedom to seek, receive and impart information and ideas of all kinds, regardless of frontiers, either orally, in writing or in print, in the form of art, or through any other media of his choice." The Human Rights Committee has further elaborated on article 19 of the ICCPR in its General Comment No. 34 which requests States to "proactively put in the public domain Government information of public interest" and "to make every effort to ensure easy, prompt, effective and practical access to such information. States parties should also enact the necessary procedures, whereby one may gain access to information, such as by means of freedom of information legislation."[15]

An extensive body of international environmental law also addresses procedural environmental rights. The best-known instrument is the *Rio Declaration on Environment and Development*[16], whose principle 10 is worth citing in full:

2003; P. CULLET, 'Definition of an Environmental Right in a Human Rights Context' (1995) 13 *Neth. Q. Hum. Rts.* (*Netherlands Quarterly of Human Rights*) 25.

13 See e.g. K. WOODS, *Human Rights and Environmental Sustainability*, Edward Elgar, Cheltenham 2010, p. 130, who argues that defending the civil and political rights of marginalized groups is key to protecting the environment.

14 OHCHR and UNEP, *Human Rights and the Environment. Rio+20: Joint Report*, United Nations, 2012, section 2.3.

15 *Id.*, paras. 18–19.

16 General Assembly, *Rio Declaration on Environment and Development*, A/CONF.151/26/Rev.1 (14 June 1992).

> *Environmental issues are best handled with participation of all concerned citizens, at the relevant level. At the national level, each individual shall have appropriate access to information concerning the environment that is held by public authorities, including information on hazardous materials and activities in their communities, and the opportunity to participate in decision-making processes. States shall facilitate and encourage public awareness and participation by making information widely available. Effective access to judicial and administrative proceedings, including redress and remedy, shall be provided.*

Although principle 10 does not characterise these procedural rights in terms of human rights, it shares similarities with a human rights approach. Perhaps the Aarhus Convention, a regional agreement that seeks to operationalize Principle 10, provides the best example of the efforts to bridge Principle 10 within a human rights framework. Its article 1 requires that State parties guarantee the rights of access to information, public participation in decision-making, and access to justice in environmental matters "in order to contribute to the protection of the right of every person of present and future generations to live in an environment adequate to his or her health and well-being."

In summary, linking existing human rights to the environment allows the use of norms that are well-established in international law to advocate for environmental protection. It also facilitates access to an array of human rights mechanisms, such as treaty bodies and human rights tribunals, to advocate for environmental protection.

B. THE RIGHT TO A HEALTHY ENVIRONMENT

Although no global binding international agreement has explicitly recognised a right to healthy[17] environment, such a right is now recognised in many national constitutions and regional instruments, with over 90 national constitutions recognising some form of environmental rights since the mid-1970s.[18] Many subnational governments also recognise

---

17 For the purposes of this article, references to a "right to a healthy environment" include all alternative formulations of such a right.

18 See D.R. BOYD, *The Environmental Rights Revolution: A Global Study of Constitutions, Human Rights, and the Environment*, University of British Columbia Press, Vancouver 2012.

such rights in the absence of their lack of recognition through a national constitution.[19]

Various regional agreements also recognise a right to a healthy environment. For example, article 24 of the 1982 African Charter on Human and Peoples' Rights provides that "all peoples shall have the right to a general satisfactory environment favourable to their development" and article 11(1) of the 1988 Additional Protocol to the American Convention on Human Rights states that "everyone shall have the right to live in a healthy environment". For further discussion, readers are referred to scholarship related to the emergence of a right to a healthy environment.[20]

III. HISTORICAL CONTEXT LEADING TO THE CREATION OF THE MANDATE

Despite the clear links established between human rights and the environment discussed in Section II, many who have been involved with this issue over the years have been frustrated at the pace of progress in further conceptually developing the relationship between these two areas at the international level.[21] The manner in which the United Nations human rights system has addressed environmental issues over the past 20 years – characterized by periods of ebbs and flows – best exemplifies the source of this frustration.

For example, despite the Stockholm Declaration's emphasis on a human right to an environment of a certain quality, the 1987 report of the World Commission on Environment and Development's recognition that "all human beings have the fundamental right to an environment adequate for their health and well-being"[22], and other post-Stockholm developments,

19 D.R. BOYD, 'The Constitutional Right to a Healthy Environment' (2012) 54:4 *Environment: Science and Policy for Sustainable Development* 3.

20 L. COLLINS, above n 2; S. ATAPATTU, above n 2; A. BOYLE, above n 12; D. SHELTON, above n 2; S.J. TURNER, *A Substantive Environmental Right: An Examination of the Legal Obligations of Decision-Makers towards the Environment*, Wolters Kluwer, Alphen aan den Rijn 2009; K.S.A. EBEKU, 'The right to a satisfactory environment and the African Commission' (2003) 3 *African Human Rights Law Journal* 149.

21 See e.g. S. ATAPATTU, above n 2.

22 World Commission on Environment and Development, *Our Common Future*, A/42/427 (4 August 1987).

the follow-up 1992 Rio Declaration took a far more muted approach by implicitly referring to the link between certain procedural rights and environmental protection and emphasizing the role of certain vulnerable groups in environmental policy making.[23] According to Alan Boyle, "the Rio Declaration's failure to give greater explicit emphasis to human rights [was] indicative of continuing uncertainty and debate about the proper place of human rights law in the development of international environmental law".[24]

In 1990, the then Sub-Commission on Prevention of Discrimination and Protection of Minorities appointed a Special Rapporteur, Mrs. Fatima Zohra Ksentini, to prepare a study of the environment and its relation to human rights. Mrs. Ksentini convened an expert meeting in Geneva to prepare draft principles on human rights and the environment (Draft Principles), which she submitted along with her final report to the Sub-Commission. Among other things, the Draft Principles stated that human rights, an ecologically sound environment, sustainable development and peace are interdependent and indivisible and that all persons have the right to a secure, healthy and ecologically sound environment. However, the Human Rights Commission did not adopt the Draft Principles.[25] Nonetheless, over the next 15 years, various bodies of the United Nations did undertake a series of actions to address the issue of human rights and the environment.

In 1995, the Human Rights Commission appointed a Special Rapporteur on the adverse effects on the enjoyment of human rights of the illicit movement

---

23 General Assembly, *Rio Declaration on Environment and Development*, A/CONF.151/26/Rev.1 (14 June 1992), principles 10, 20–23; see also A. BOYLE, above n 12, at 473–474; S. ATAPATTU, above n 2, at 74–78.

24 A. BOYLE, 'The role of International Human Rights Law in the Protection of the Environment' in A. BOYLE and M. ANDERSON (eds.), *Human Rights Approaches to Environmental Protection*, Oxford University Press, Oxford 1996; see also D. SHELTON, 'What Happened in Rio to Human Rights?' (1992) 3 *Y.B. of Int'l Env't L* (*Yearbook of International Environmental Law*) 75, 82.

25 See e.g. K. WOLFE, 'Greening the International Human Rights Sphere? Environmental Rights and the Draft Declaration of Principles on Human Rights and the Environment' (2003) 9 *Appeal: rev. Current L. & L. Reform* (*Appeal: Review of Current Law & Law Reform*) 45, 48 (noting that as of the date of publication, "there has been no movement on any of Ksentini's recommendations, nor have the final report or the *Draft Declaration* been substantively discussed. Efforts to incite discussion on the *Draft Declaration* by NGOs have been wholly unsuccessful").

and dumping of toxic and dangerous products and wastes, a mandate that still continues under the Human Rights Council.[26]

Subsequently, in 2002, at the request of the Commission on Human Rights, the OHCHR and UNEP convened a joint meeting of experts on human rights and the environment "to review and assess progress achieved since [the Rio Conference] in promoting and protecting human rights in relation to environmental questions."[27]

Next, the Commission on Human Rights in its decision 2004/19 requested the Secretary-General to submit a report "on the consideration being given to the relationship between the environment and human rights as part of sustainable development." The Secretary General's report reviews developments at the international, regional and national level recognising the link between human rights and the environment.[28]

Starting in 2008, the HRC began adopting a series of resolutions concerning climate change, paving the way for a renewed focus on developing the linkage of human rights and the environment. To begin with, the Human Rights Council in Resolution 7/23, among other things, requested OHCHR to conduct a detailed analytical study on the relationship between climate change and human rights, taking account the views of States and other stakeholders. Also for the first time in a UN resolution, the HRC stated that climate change "poses an immediate and far-reaching threat to people and communities around the world and has implications for the full enjoyment of human rights."

OHCHR submitted its report in January 2009, and in addition to providing a useful outline of the relationship between the environment and human rights and the implications of climate change on specific rights, the report

26 Commission on Human Rights, *Adverse effects of the illicit movement and dumping of toxic and dangerous products and wastes on the enjoyment of human rights*, E/CN.4/RES/1995/81 (8 March 1995); the Resolution requests that the Special Rapporteur, among other things, investigate and examine the effects of the illicit dumping of toxic and dangerous products and wastes in African and other developing countries on the enjoyment of human rights, in particular on the human rights to life and health of everyone.

27 Commission of Human Rights, *Science and the Environment*, E/CN.4/DEC/2001/111 (25 April 2001).

28 Commission on Human Rights, *Human rights and the environment as part of sustainable development*, E/CN.4/2005/96 (19 January 2005).

discusses various State obligations relevant to addressing or mitigating climate change.[29] Importantly, the OHCHR report concluded that climate change can be effectively addressed through the obligations of international cooperation, an obligation that is central to the realization of human rights.[30]

In March 2009, taking into consideration the finding of the OHCHR climate change report, the HRC adopted Resolution 10/4 on human rights and climate change, noting that climate-change related effects have a range of direct and indirect implications for the effective enjoyment of human rights. The Resolution also called for a panel discussion on the relationship between climate change and human rights, which took place in June 2009.[31] By this point, according to one participant, "no delegation argued with the notion that climate change has implications for a wide range of explicitly identified, internationally protected human rights."[32]

Subsequently, from 29 November to 1 December 2009 the United Nations Environmental Programme and OHCHR organised a high-level expert meeting on the future of human rights and environment. The outcome document recognized that the recent attention given to human rights in relationship to climate change highlighted the need to better clarify and develop the links between human rights and environment, including "looking at the obligations and responsibilities of States and other actors under human rights treaties and multilateral environmental agreements and assessing and re-examining how human rights bear on environmental problems and environmental governance in an operational manner."[33]

---

29 Report of the Office of the United Nations High Commissioner for Human Rights, *The relationship between climate change and human rights*, A/HRC/10/61 (15 January 2009).

30 See also J.H. KNOX, above n 2.

31 See OHCHR, *Human Rights Council panel discussion on the relationship between climate change and human rights: summary of discussions* (15 June 2009) available at www.ohchr.org/EN/Issues/HRAndClimateChange/Pages/Panel.aspx (last accessed on 15 February 2015).

32 E. CAMERON and M. LIMON, 'Restoring the Climate by Realizing Rights: The Role of the International Human Rights System' (2012) 21:3 *RECIEL* (*Review of European Community & International Environmental Law*) 204, 208.

33 UNEP/OHCHR, *Outcome Document of the High Level Expert Meeting on the New future of Human Rights and Environment: An Agenda for Moving Forward* (1 December 2009) available at www.unep.org/environmentalgovernance/Portals/8/documents/Events/OutcomeDocumentHumanRightsEnviroment.pdf (last accessed on 15 February 2015).

In March 2011, the Human Rights Council requested the OHCHR to prepare a detailed analytical study on the relationship between human rights and the environment. The study, which was submitted in December 2011, provided a broad overview of how national, regional, and internal human rights law mechanisms have addressed the connection between human rights and the environment.[34]

In October 2011, the HRC adopted another resolution on human rights and climate change (Resolution 18/22), in which it requested the OHCHR to convene a seminar on addressing the adverse impacts of climate change on the enjoyment of human rights and to submit a summary report of such seminar. The seminar took place on 23–24 February 2012.

As explained above, the mandate of the Independent Expert on human right and environment was established by the HRC in March 2012. For many experts and organisations which had been involved with human rights and environment issues over the years, the establishment of the mandate was long overdue. Nonetheless, the mandate provides the opportunity to clarify and build consensus around the human rights obligations related to the protection of the environment.[35]

IV. THE PRELIMINARY REPORT OF THE INDEPENDENT EXPERT

The Independent Expert submitted his first report to the HRC at its 22nd session in February-March 2013.[36] According to the Independent Expert, the preliminary report is "intended to place the mandate in a historical context, present some of the outstanding issues relevant to the relationship between human rights and the environment and describe the current and planned programme of activities".[37]

---

34 UN High Commissioner for Human Rights, *Analytical study on the relationship between human rights and the environment*, A/HRC/19/34 (16 December 2011).

35 See E. CAMERON and M. LIMON, above n 32, at 212.

36 Report of the Independent Expert on the issue of human rights obligations relating to the enjoyment of a safe, clean, healthy and sustainable environment, *Preliminary report*, A/HRC/22/43 (24 December 2012).

37 *Id.* para. 6.

The Independent Expert recognises that human rights and environmental protection are inherently interdependent, and that the development of this relationship has primarily taken two forms: namely through the adoption of an explicit right to an environment and through heightened attention to the relationship between the environment with already recognised human rights.[38] Nonetheless, despite clear progress in developing linkages between the two areas, the report explains that many issues related to the obligations that human rights law imposes regarding environmental protection need greater study and clarification. Indeed, the Independent Expert views this study and clarification as the principal focus of this mandate.[39]

According to the report, a non-exhaustive list of areas requiring further clarification includes:

> *the relationship between human rights obligations and best practices; the connections between substantive and procedural rights and duties; vulnerable groups and non-discrimination; human rights obligations relating to transboundary and global environmental harm; the application of human rights norms to non-State actors; and the relationship between a right to a healthy environment and other human rights.*[40]

Other issues that the Independent Expert believes may deserve closer examination include "the potential rights of future generations; the application of human rights obligations to especially pressing environmental challenges, including climate change, armed conflict and the environmentally displaced, and ... the relevance of human rights to protection of non-human aspects of the environment."[41]

V. CONCLUSION

The establishment of the mandate of the Independent Expert on human rights and the environment must be placed with the broader context of the evolution of environmental rights. Although much has been done to develop the relationship between human rights and the environment in

38 *Id.*, para. 10–11.
39 *Id.*, para. 35.
40 *Id.*, para. 36.
41 *Id.*, para. 53.

different forums, there remain many issues that require further attention. The establishment of this mandate provides the opportunity to clarify difficult legal issues and to build consensus among the wide range of actors that have been following and contributing to this issue over the years.

THE MANDATE OF THE UN WORKING GROUP ON BUSINESS AND HUMAN RIGHTS: PRELIMINARY THOUGHTS

Michael K. Addo*

I. INTRODUCTION

The United Nations has been on a long search for an effective policy strategy for addressing issues raised by human rights in the conduct of business.[1] The year 2005 marked an important turning point in that enquiry when the United Nations Commission on Human Rights (replaced in 2006 by the Human Rights Council)[2] requested the UN Secretary General to appoint a Special Representative to "identify and clarify standards of corporate responsibility and accountability with regard to human rights".[3] This task fell to Professor John Ruggie who proposed, in 2008, a policy framework known as the Protect, Respect, and Remedy Framework.[4] This policy framework was based on three structural pillars, firstly, the State duty to protect against human rights abuses by third parties including business enterprises; secondly the responsibility of business enterprises to respect human rights which entails business to avoid infringing on the human rights of others and thirdly the need for access to effective remedy for

* Chairperson/Rapporteur of the UN Working Group on the Issue of Human Rights and Transnational Corporations and Other Business Enterprises.

1 For a summary review of some of these initiatives, see Report of the United Nations High Commissioner on Human Rights on the Responsibilities of Transnational Corporations and Related Business Enterprises with Regard to Human Rights, UN. Doc. E/CN.4/2005/91 (15 February 2005).

2 General Assembly, *Human Rights Council*, A/RES/60/251 (15 March 2006).

3 Commission on Human Rights, *Human rights and transnational corporations and other business enterprises*, Res. 2005/69 (20 April 2005).

4 Report of the Special Representative of the Secretary-General on the issue of human rights and transnational corporations and other business enterprises, *Protect, Respect and Remedy: A Framework for Business and Human Rights*, A/HRC/8/5 (7 April 2008).

anyone whose rights are violated or adversely affected.[5] The three pillars are at once independent and complementary at the same time and according to Ruggie, "[E]ach principle is an essential component of the framework: the State duty to protect because it lies at the core of the international human rights regime; the corporate responsibility to respect because it is the basic expectation society has of business; and access to remedy, because even the most concerted efforts cannot prevent all abuse".[6] This policy framework was very well received by the Council on account of which it renewed Ruggie's mandate in order for him to propose ways of operationalizing the policy framework.

In 2011 he submitted his final report in which he presented the Guiding Principles on Business and Human Rights: Implementing the United Nations "Protect, Respect and Remedy" Framework.[7] This document contains 31 different principles with commentaries elaborating on ways of operationalizing the three pillars proposed in the Protect, Respect and Remedy framework.[8]

At its 18th session in 2011, the United Nations Human Rights Council marked another important milestone in its evolving policy strategy for human rights and business with the election of a Working Group of five independent experts to determine the future direction of this subject. This development presents valuable opportunities as well as critical challenges. This article reviews the opportunities and challenges presented by the terms of the mandate of the Working Group on Business and Human Rights.

---

5 *Id.*

6 *Id.*, par. 9. For a review of the development of the Framework, see K. BUHMANN, 'The Development of the 'UN Framework': A Pragmatic Process Towards a Pragmatic Output' in R. MARES (ed.), *The UN Guiding Principles on Business and Human Rights: Foundations and Implementation*, Nijhoff, Leiden 2012, p. 85.

7 Report of the Special Representative of the Secretary-General on the issue of human rights and transnational corporations and other business enterprises, *Guiding Principles on Business and Human Rights: Implementing the United Nations "Protect, Respect and Remedy" Framework*, A/HRC/17/31 (21 March 2011).

8 See R. MARES, 'Business and Human Rights After Ruggie: Foundations, the Art of Simplification and the Imperative of Cumulative Process' in R. MARES (ed.), *The UN Guiding Principles on Business and Human Rights: Foundations and Implementation*, Nijhoff, Leiden 2012.

II. THE MANDATE OF THE WORKING GROUP

In its resolution 17/4,[9] the Human Rights Council mandated the Working Group on Business and Human Rights inter alia:

(a) To promote the effective and comprehensive dissemination and implementation of the Guiding Principles;
(b) To identify, exchange and promote good practices and lessons learned on the implementation of the Guiding Principles and to assess and make recommendations thereon and, in that context, to seek and receive information from all relevant sources, including Governments, transnational corporations and other business enterprises, national human rights institutions, civil society and rights-holders;
(c) To provide support for efforts to promote capacity-building and the use of the Guiding Principles, as well as, upon request, to provide advice and recommendations regarding the development of domestic legislation and policies relating to business and human rights;
(d) To conduct country visits and to respond promptly to invitations from States;
(e) To continue to explore options and make recommendations at the national, regional and international levels for enhancing access to effective remedies available to those whose human rights are affected by corporate activities, including those in conflict areas;
(f) To integrate a gender perspective throughout the work of the mandate and to give special attention to persons living in vulnerable situations, in particular children;
(g) To work in close cooperation and coordination with other relevant special procedures of the Human Rights Council, relevant United Nations and other international bodies, the treaty bodies and regional human rights organizations;
(h) To develop a regular dialogue and discuss possible areas of cooperation with Governments and all relevant actors, including relevant United Nations bodies, specialized agencies, funds and programmes, in particular the Office of the United Nations High Commissioner for Human Rights, the Global Compact, the International Labour Organization, the World Bank and its International Finance

9 Human Rights Council, *Human rights and transnational corporations and other business enterprises*, A/HRC/RES/17/4 (6 July 2011).

Corporation, the United Nations Development Programme and the International Organization for Migration, as well as transnational corporations and other business enterprises, national human rights institutions, representatives of indigenous peoples, civil society organizations and other regional and subregional international organizations;

(i) To guide the work of the Forum on Business and Human Rights established pursuant to paragraph 12 below;

(j) To report annually to the Human Rights Council and the General Assembly.[10]

There is no doubt that this is a truly exciting mandate but one that is not so easy to implement. The first on the list of tasks for the Working Group to promote the effective and comprehensive dissemination and implementation of the Guiding Principles alone demands engagement with no less that 193 countries and no less that 8 million transnational corporations and their subsidiaries.[11] To this, one may add the expectation of other bodies and groups such as business associations, professional bodies, non-governmental organisations, civil society groups, potential and actual victims of business activities, etc., to work with the Working Group in the dissemination and implementation of the Guiding Principles. Any of the other nine additional tasks set out in the mandate entail similar if more effort on the part of the Working Group. In effect thus, the mandate of the Working Group cannot be taken literally or else it will be impossible to carry out. The enormity and complexity of the mandate call for an imaginative and strategic approach to its implementation.

In being imaginative and strategic, the Working Group has been mindful of certain pragmatic and compelling considerations. Firstly, the Working Group has placed itself within the wide and evolving space of human rights and business in the definition of its role. This role is informed by the circumstances in which the Working Group finds itself reflecting the time and resources available to the Working Group and the goodwill of stakeholders, including States, business entities and civil society groups to

---

10 *Id.*, para. 6.

11 Report of the Special Representative of the Secretary-General on the issue of human rights and transnational corporations and other business enterprises, *Business and human rights: Further steps toward the operationalization of the "protect, respect and remedy" framework*, A/HRC/14/27 (9 April 2010), para. 82.

support the work of the Working Group. In this respect, it is also important for the Working Group to appreciate that the mandate and the tasks set out as part of it is a long term objective to which this and subsequent mandate holders will contribute. Setting realistic and measurable targets are important considerations if the Working Group is to make a meaningful contribution to the development of UN policy on human rights and business.

Another important consideration for the Working Group has been to be faithful to the text of its mandate. The Human Rights Council has not been unaware of the enormity of the task it laid out in the mandate but it has also been careful in the role expected of the Working Group. According to the establishing resolution, the Working Group is expected to promote, identify, exchange, support, to explore options and to guide.[12] This suggests, firstly, that the primary actors under the mandate are other stakeholders such as States and business entities and secondly, that the mandate given to the Working Group is not a command and control one. Both considerations are not insignificant in view of the fact that the Guiding Principles around which the Working Group mandate is set are directed at these key actors. In addition, one of the important lessons from the Ruggie years is the virtue of consultation and cooperation among stakeholders in the development of emerging standards. During his mandate John Ruggie held forty-seven multi-stakeholder consultations across all continents and made site visits to business operations in over twenty countries.[13] This is in addition to the extensive on-line consultations throughout his mandate. Ruggie also worked closely with stakeholders to undertake research into difficult and unsettled issues such as the human rights and business in conflict-affected regions,[14] principles of responsible contracts,[15] resolving methodological

---

12 *Id.*

13 Report of the Special Representative of the Secretary-General on the issue of human rights and transnational corporations and other business enterprises, *Guiding Principles on Business and Human Rights: Implementing the United Nations "Protect, Respect and Remedy" Framework*, A/HRC/17/31 (21 March 2011), para. 8.

14 Report of the Special Representative of the Secretary-General on the issue of human rights and transnational corporations and other business enterprises, *Business and human rights in conflict-affected regions: challenges and options towards State responses*, A/HRC/17/32 (27 May 2011).

15 Report of the Special Representative of the Secretary-General on the issue of human rights and transnational corporations and other business enterprises,

issues in the conduct of human rights impact assessments,[16] the extent to which business recognizes human rights,[17] corporate responsibility under international law and issues in extra-territorial regulation[18] and many more. These reports helped to define common understanding of the issues raised by the subject of human rights and business but also to "help[ed] inform Human Rights Council debates, nudge protagonists to moderate their more excessive claims, and provide a strong foundation for [the SRSG] to build on."[19]

Admittedly, the lack of a coercive mandate for the Working Group with which to compel actions of stakeholders may seem like a weakness but as John Ruggie demonstrated throughout his mandate the cooperative approach may in fact also be a valuable strength if applied creatively. John Ruggie turned a simple and bland mandate into a successful strategy that he termed principled pragmatism, defined as:

> *[A]n unflinching commitment to the principle of strengthening the promotion and protection of human rights as it relates to business, coupled with a pragmatic attachment to what works best in creating change where it matters most – in the daily lives of people.*[20]

This process was subsequently elaborated as seeking to achieve the maximum reduction in corporate-related human rights harm in the

Principles for Responsible Contracts: Integrating the management of human rights risks into State-investor contract negotiations, A/HRC/17/31/Add.3 (25 May 2011).

16 Report of the Special Representative of the Secretary-General on the issue of human rights and transnational corporations and other business enterprises, *Human rights impact assessments: Resolving key methodological questions*, A/HRC/4/74 (5 February 2007).

17 Report of the Special Representative of the Secretary-General on the issue of human rights and transnational corporations and other business enterprises, *Business recognition of human rights; Global patterns, regional and sectoral variations*, A/HRC/4/35/Add.4 (8 February 2007).

18 Report of the Special Representative of the Secretary-General on the issue of human rights and transnational corporations and other business enterprises, *Corporate responsibility under international law and issues in extraterritorial regulation: summary of legal workshops*, A/HRC/4/35/Add.2 (15 February 2007).

19 Business & Human Rights Resource Centre, available at www.business-humanrights.org/SpecialRepPortal/Home (last accessed on 15 February 2015).

20 Report of the Special Representative of the Secretary-General on the issue of human rights and transnational corporations and other business enterprises, *Interim Report*, E/CN.4/2006/97 (22 February 2006), para. 81.

shortest possible period of time, by establishing a common platform for action on which cumulative progress could be built, without foreclosing any promising longer-term developments.[21]

In practice, this firm and unequivocal commitment to the effective protection of human rights coupled with the search for a common platform of action involved a transparent and participatory process involving an intensive and rigorous process of multi-stakeholder consultations, research as well as an active engagement with his critics. The outcome of Ruggie's approach to developing the Guiding Principles was a regime that is evidence-based and draws on the perspectives of most if not all stakeholders into a shared understanding of the roles and expectations of all stakeholders. The effect of this has been a sense of inclusiveness and ownership of the Guiding Principles by all interests.

III. THE STRATEGY OF THE WORKING GROUP

One year since its appointment, the Working Group has held two sessions, submitted its report to the Human Rights Council and to the General Assembly and preparing to guide its first Annual Forum. In this time, it has noted some important considerations that have helped to develop its priorities and strategy including:

- ensuring that the Guiding Principles provide a common point of reference for all stakeholders;
- the need for access by victims of business-related human rights abuse to effective remedies;
- to cultivate an environment conducive to the dissemination and implementation of the Guiding Principles.[22]

21 John Ruggie, *Lecture for Sir Geoffrey Chandler Speaker Series* (Royal Society for the Encouragement of Arts, Manufacturers and Commerce), London, 11 January 2011, available at http://business-humanrights.org/sites/default/files/media/documents/ruggie/john-ruggie-presentation-at-rsa-in-london-11-jan-2011.pdf (Last accessed on 15 February 2015).

22 Report of the Working Group on the issue of human rights and transnational corporations and other business enterprises, A/HRC/20/29 (10 April 2012), para. 48.

It has become evident that there is an acute lack of awareness of the Guiding Principles among the vast majority of stakeholders. The unanimous endorsement of the Guiding Principles a year earlier did not seem, by itself, to translate into broad awareness on the ground. This makes the dissemination task and its identification as a strategic consideration a matter of priority. For this objective, the Working Group proposes to reach new audiences, that is to say, stakeholders who are not yet aware of the content and implications of the Guiding Principle by partnering with 'multipliers' and 'catalysts'.[23] These are networks and institutions such as business associations, development agencies, and regional institutions. For this objective, the Working Group undertakes:

> *to prioritize its engagement with those governance frameworks that (a) have an effective accountability mechanisms; (b) can demonstrate a track record of adherence by [its] members/participants to their tenets; (c) apply to a large number of actors; and (d)provide effective grievance mechanism for affected individuals.*[24]

This emphasis on 'active and successful' governance institutions is not to suggest that the less dynamic institutions do not feature in the strategy of the Working Group. Such institutions may not lie in the field of priority of Working Group activity at this stage but continue to play a role in the wider implementation of the Guiding Principles.

This emphasis in the Working Group strategy on active and successful governance regimes carries a risk of looking up to Western developed country institutions such as the European Union, the Organisation of Economic Cooperation and Development (OECD) and the Council of Europe. This poses the question of whether this undermines the integrity of the work of the Working Group in any way. This is unlikely to be the case because it does not necessarily follow that the search for a governance regime with the characteristics listed above will exclude mechanisms from the global South. The African Commission on Human and Peoples' Rights for example has demonstrated the success that justifies Working Group attention in this regard. Furthermore, the focus should lie with the qualitative value that such an emphasis is likely to deliver to the activities of the Working Group. Such an emphasis on the active and successful institutions, regardless of geographical origin, is likely to produce the good practices that may be

23 *Id.*, para. 64.
24 *Id.*, para. 72.

shared with other actors and stakeholder. Also, working with institutions with established accountability mechanisms, successful grievance regimes etc allows the Working Group to strategically complement its activities with the processes of these institutions in order to deliver tangible results in areas such as redress where its own mandate is weak.

The Working Group represents the dissemination strategy as a means to a comprehensive implementation rather than as an end in itself and for this objective it is able to focus on new audiences as a matter of priority. This is not to suggest that established stakeholders are not important. Rather, actors who are fully aware of the Guiding Principles generate entirely different issues for the attention of the Working Group, such as the risks of fragmentation in the application of the Guiding Principles.

A. CONVERGENCE

The relatively small constituency of stakeholders who are aware of the Guiding Principles have began to implement and apply them at different speeds and according to their own understanding. That stakeholders have been proactive is commendable but this unintegrated application risks fragmentation of the regime. It has been argued, rightly, that the Guiding principles are not meant to be a one size fits all.[25] In a world of 80,000 transnational corporations and 10 times as many subsidiaries, and not to mention national firms seeking to construct guidelines that fit all will be unrealistic if not impossible. The aim of the Guiding principles is to provide universally applicable benchmarks that allow companies to apply them in different circumstances taking account of the complexity of tools and processes that companies employ.[26]

In the same way, as the Guiding Principles are not intended as a took kit to be taken off the shelf and applied blindly,[27] they do not represent "a

25 United Nations, *Business and human rights: Further steps toward the operationalization of the "protect, respect and remedy" framework*. Report of the SRSG on the Issue of Human Rights and Transnational Corporations and Other Business Enterprises. UN Doc. A/HRC/14/27 (1010) para. 82.

26 *Ibid.* [A/HRC/14/27).

27 United Nations, *Guiding Principles on Business and Human Rights, loc. cit.* para. 15.

silver bullet solution to the institutional misalignments in the business and human rights domain. Instead, all social actors – States, businesses, and civil society – must learn to do many things differently".[28] The inherent flexibility of the Guiding Principles must be acknowledged but it is important that the Working Group asserts its position as the central focus for authoritative interpretation of the Guiding Principles.

In its strategy for the implementation of its mandate the Working Group is keen to promote convergence, consistency and coordination in the application of the Guiding Principles. According to the Working Group:

> *The Guiding Principles are the point towards which existing and future human rights and business standards and related tools, guidelines, resources, services and initiatives for companies and States should converge. The Guiding Principles should remain the authoritative basis of understanding of the respective responsibilities and duties of business enterprises and States, and how these should be operationalized in practice. This objective should be pursued without curtailing further enhancement of standards or extension of expectations beyond the benchmark provided by the Guiding principles.*[29]

In this respect the Working Group is keen to prevent duplication of initiatives as well as "avoiding repetition, fragmentation and digression" among existing users of the Guiding Principles.[30] To successfully deliver on these undertakings, the Working Group has to provide strategic leadership and for this it has committed itself to developing interpretative tools as well as "articulate indicators for processes and outcomes by which all stakeholders may assess for themselves the effectiveness of … existing and emerging tools."[31]

There is no power under the mandate for the Working Group to issue directives that may normally be seem as encompassing directives on the scope and meaning of the Guiding Principles. Yet, by their broad and general nature the Guiding Principles will need further interpretation in their application in the variety of contexts where they are applicable. For the Working Group, the promotion of implementation requires a certain

28 United Nations, *Business and Human Rights: Further steps, loc. cit.*, para. 5.
29 Report of the Working Group, *loc. cit.*, para. 49.
30 *Ibid.*, para. 51.
31 *Ibid.*, paras. 52–54.

understanding of what is to be promoted within a particular context. So also is interpretation necessary for the identification of good practices that is to be promoted among stakeholders. The language of the establishing resolution therefore enables the Working Group to claim to be the ultimate guardian of the integrity of the Guiding Principles. In the absence of coercive powers, it may need a deliberate and conscious method for asserting this authority and encouraging stakeholders to accept their status. The convergence that the Working Group craves and which the terms of the mandate support is, no doubt, an important virtue but may need careful crafting to achieve, especially if it cannot justifiably be decreed by the Working Group.

B. HOLISTIC STANDARDS

Another important consideration for the Working Group in crafting its strategy and defining its priorities is to affirm the holistic nature of the Guiding Principles and interdependent character of its three Pillars. It is understandable that individual stakeholders may be tempted to focus their attention on particular pillars where their interest and expertise lie. States may tend to address pillar I issues while business entities may wish to focus on pillar II issues and civil society groups and non-governmental organisations tending to work with pillars II and III. However, this should be done with a clear appreciation of the implications of other pillars without expecting that business entities will assume pillar I responsibilities. The terms of this integrated approach remain unclear in the strategy of the Working Group at the present time and need further development at a later date.

C. INDIVIDUAL COMMUNICATIONS

One pressing question with the mandate of the Working group is what to do with individual communications. There is no express mandate for the Working Group to consider such communications but potential and actual victims have and will continue to bring allegations of adverse human rights impacts by business entities and the Working Group need not feel out of its depth on such communications as there are diverse opportunities under the mandate to employ such information in the development of its priorities as well as to enhance other tasks under the mandate. Information from individual communication may form the basis for the identification, exchange and promotion of good practices and lessons learned[32] or for the determination of priorities for capacity building[33] or indeed in the selection of countries where country visits[34] may be fruitful. Information from individual communications may also form the basis for exploring options and making recommendations at the national, regional and international levels for enhancing access to effective remedies for affected individuals and groups.[35]

The subject of access to effective remedy features highly in the strategy of the Working Group in terms of recognizing its importance to the effective implementation of the Guiding Principles. According to the Working Group strategy for the implementation of its mandate, it hopes to promote human rights accountability of business enterprises and of States by ensuring the uptake of the Guiding Principles by international and regional accountability mechanisms.[36] For a mandate that does not have an express authority to consider communication the link with existing regimes that are able to provide redress is especially important. Consequently, the adoption of the Guiding Principles by governance institutions such as the OECD, the ILO, regional human rights institutions is likely to be an important anchor for the successful implementation of the mandate of the Working Group.

A successful strategy on the significance of communications is critical to the success of this mandate but it poses the most obvious risks of backlash from the different stakeholders if it is not handled imaginatively. Lessons from other Special Procedure mandate holders and the practice of the United Nations under the procedures of the former Commission on Human Rights and now under those of the Human Rights Council over the past decades may be especially useful. The best answers to the issues posed by this matter may lie in a long term strategy of open and continuous learning and sharing of knowledge rather than a short term policy based on limited experience.

---

32 Resolution 17/4 (2011) *loc. cit.* para. 6(b).
33 *Ibid.*, para. 6(c).
34 *Ibid.*, para. 6(d).
35 *Ibid.*, para. 6(e).
36 Report of the Working Group *loc. cit.*, para. 58.

D. THE BUSINESS CASE

The promotion of the business case for human rights is listed in the Working Group strategy for the implementation of its mandate.[37] This is an interesting subject but an extremely complex one that calls for further elaboration by the Working Group.

Although the phrase "the business case" has found its way into the common parlance of the business and human rights discourse, its precise meaning is uncertain as different constituencies tend to mean different things by the 'business case'. For some, the business case refers to the beneficial value – tangible or intangible – that business may derive from the adoption and application of a social policy initiative such as the UN Guiding Principles. This understanding of the concept is premised on the representation of social policy initiatives as external to the conduct of business. Their application of social policy guidelines is therefore not normally expected of business and if these social norms are to be adopted it has to be driven by identified corresponding or compensating benefit, preferably defined in terms of economic value. This view of the business case is founded on a neo-liberal view of conducting business and guided by market forces that determine the optimum economic equilibrium. According to this approach, social policies such as human rights tend to distort the equilibrium of the market and the credibility of the profit from the conduct of business and therefore should be avoided if at all possible. If business is called upon to take account of social factors, then this has to be justified in terms of alternative value.

For others, the meaning of the concept of the business case is much more nuanced and scoped around the compelling reasons for applying yet another regime of non-binding guidelines. This view of the business case does not object to the significance of social factors in the conduct of business in principle. It accommodates social factors as part of essential external (often governmental) regulation of business. From this point of view, the business case is defined against the context of recognized directives to business enterprises. In a hierarchy of such directions, those defined by the law are considered compelling while non-law directives are open to the discretion of the enterprise. In this sense, the human rights standards

37 *Ibid.*, para. 62.

such as the prohibition of discrimination in employment or in the provision of services that are grounded in legal directives have to be complied with. Whilst this may not necessarily be the case for non-legal directives, different justifications may be put forward for acceding to this latter category of non-binding directives, including under certain circumstances the benefits to be gained by the enterprise when implementing such directives. Similarly, strategic factors such as developing a social image alongside a brand or seeking to be ethical or philanthropic could be good reasons for implementing non-binding directives. While appreciating the significance of social factors such as human rights in the conduct of economic undertakings the business case from this perspective carries the handicap of inconsistency as different enterprises, or sectors apply different standards depending upon which factors are rated as sufficiently compelling.

For yet another rendition of the concept of the business case for the application of social factors whether and whatever business may gain from human rights, either as a binding or non-binding regime, the focus may be laid on seeking to identify what is so special about the body of social norms such as the UN Guiding Principles, the UN Global Compact[38] or the OECD Guidelines for Multinational Enterprise.[39] The special character may be based on the alignment of the values that underlie the social standards with those of the business vision or simply that the process used for the adoption of the social standards make them an uniquely integral part of the business approach to the conduct of its affairs. This is an imprecise approach to the application of social standards to the conduct of business and yet may strengthen a credible and sustainable business case.

The various representation of the idea of a business case are related and therefore, in practice, a credible business case may need to respond to all the questions and uncertainties raised by the different understandings of the concept of a business case. Herein lies the difficulty with the whole idea of conceiving of a business case for the UN Guiding Principles. By their very nature, the Guiding Principles as guidelines speak flexibly to different business communities and so making it difficult to conceive of a standard business case. If a case is to be made it may have to be one of many cases designed to suit different business environments, contexts and times.

---

38 Www.unglobalcompact.org.

39 Www.oecd.org/daf/internationalinvestment/guidelinesformultinationalenterprises/.

E. STRATEGIC PARTNERSHIPS

With the Working Group's strategic emphasis on multi-stakeholder consultations and its heavy leanings on other institutions to provide support for access to remedy, a casual assessment of the strategy of the Working Group may give the impression of an excessive dependence on others in the implementation of its mandate. Such a view cannot however be justified on a careful assessment of the nature of the mandate. Reference has already been made above to the target of the object of the Guiding Principles being other stakeholders with the Working Group in a more secondary promotional and facilitative role rather than a command and control authority. Its secondary role is however not insignificant as it is expected to provide leadership and act as the point of convergence in the interpretation and application of the Guiding Principles. In the same vein, it should be obvious even to the most casual observer that it is nigh impossible for a group of five experts working part-time on such a complex mandate to successfully undertake the necessary tasks on their own. The numbers of potential actors that need to be reached has been mentioned above but this can be made even more daunting if one looked at the nature of the tasks that such interaction may entail. Consider, as an example, the capacity building expectations of this mandate and the Working Group could easily be overwhelmed if it undertook to deliver this on its own. It necessarily therefore lends itself to drawing on the contribution of others especially if the others happen to be in the best position to undertake particular tasks.

Furthermore, there are good lessons from the Ruggie era that suggest that the inclusive and participatory approach coupled with full transparency in the work of the Working Group is especially rewarding. Not only does it engage the key actors but it provides the opportunity to determine and reflect common understanding of the issues. For the Working Group therefore, the partnership with other actors and stakeholders in the delivery of its mandate is both strategic and functional.

In any case, there are specific tasks that cannot be undertaken by anyone else other than the Working Group itself. These include undertaking country visits, working in collaboration with UN bodies, Funds and agencies as well as guiding the annual Forum. In addition, the Working Group has adopted a hands-on approach to the implementation of its mandate by launching a number of 'projects' of its own, the aim of which is to maintain a direct role in the development of the mandate. The projects have been carefully identified to touch on the key priorities of the mandate and so to enable the Working Group to remain in contact with the activities of all stakeholders. The projects include:

- Support Governments in the elaboration and implementation of national plans of action designed to implement the State duty to protect human rights, in relation to business activities and their impacts;
- Raise awareness of the Guiding Principles and promote their implementation in the context of the activities of extractive industry enterprises, particularly with regard to access to effective remedies;
- Promote convergence in the implementation and interpretation of the Guiding Principles with regard to access to effective remedy by developing further guidance on the elements of effective remedy;
- Identify strategic opportunities to further embed the Guiding Principles into global governance frameworks;
- Support implementation of the Guiding Principles by fostering peer discussion and learning among States and business enterprises on experiences.[40]

Each of these projects is expected to be led by a Working Group member or a team of members designed with specific outcomes in mind. Most will provide tools and guidelines that stakeholders may employ in the further development of the contributions to the mandate.

IV. CONCLUSION

The United Nations policy on human rights and business can be said to be fairly well settled and attention has shifted to realizing the ideals set out in the PRR Framework and the Guiding Principles. This makes the mandate of the Working Group on Business and Human Rights particularly significant. While it is able to draw on lessons from the past it is embarking on an unrehearsed undertaking in which there is high level of interest form all stakeholders. At the same time, experience suggests that the Working Group is not operating in isolation and benefits from the support of all stakeholders as a result of the participatory multi-stakeholder approach to implementation.

40 See Report of the Working Group to the General Assembly (2012).

There is an unequivocal need for convergence and common understanding and it is up to the Working Group to assert the role of primary guardian of the integrity of the Guiding Principles. In the absence of coercive powers the Working Group will require all of its powers of diplomacy and persuasion to maintain the confidence of all the stakeholders.

Success in the implementation of the mandate depends on awareness across stakeholder groups. After one year of its mandate, the Working group still identifies the lack of awareness as a major challenge. Its dissemination strategy needs further attention and the first annual Forum scheduled for December 2012 will go a long way to address this challenge.

ON THE TWENTIETH ANNIVERSARY OF THE UNITED NATIONS DECLARATION FOR THE PROTECTION OF ALL PERSONS AGAINST ENFORCED DISAPPEARANCES

Olivier DE FROUVILLE*

I. INTRODUCTION

The Declaration for the Protection of All Persons Against Enforced Disappearances turned twenty years old in 2012. This international instrument is closely linked to the UN Working Group on Enforced or Involuntary Disappearances, the special procedure of the Human Rights Council tasked with examining this issue at the universal level.

It should be recalled that the Working Group was created in 1980, as a response to the plight of families of disappeared persons, mainly in Latin America. For more than 30 years now, it has been mandated by States to act as a humanitarian "channel of communication" between governments and families, with a view to ascertain the fate or the whereabouts of the disappeared.

In the first ten years, the Working Group has received thousands of new cases, not only from the countries of Latin America, but from all over the world. The Working Group helped to uncover the fact that enforced disappearances was being used as a practice of terror against civilian

* Member of the UN Human Rights Committee; former Member and Chair-of the UN Working Group on Enforced of Involuntary Disappearances (2008–2014). Professor at Université Panthéon-Assas (Paris II), and Director of the Research Centre on Human Rights and Humanitarian Law (CRDH) of the same institution. I wish to thank Humberto Cantú Rivera for his translation and editing of this article.

populations in a number of countries, generally in situations of serious crisis or armed conflict. The Working Group also made tremendous efforts to improve the identification of the phenomenon from a legal point of view. Its work paved the way for the adoption of the *Declaration* by the General Assembly on 18th of December 1992. From this moment, the Working Group was tasked by the Commission on Human Rights to monitor the progress made by States in the implementation of the standards of the Declaration.

While promoting the Declaration, the Working Group fully supported the drafting of the new Convention. It advocated the creation of an autonomous Committee, knowing from the beginning that the work of such a Committee would complement and strengthen the efforts of the Working Group. While waiting for the adoption and universal ratification of the Convention, the Declaration provided and continues to provide an invaluable guide for States to prevent enforced disappearances, to punish those who commit them and to repair the consequences. The Declaration is a *complete* instrument, one that fully seizes the specificity of the crime of enforced disappearance as a negation of the legal personality of an individual, as well as the specificity of the suffering inflicted upon the families and other persons close to the disappeared. With the Declaration, the inexpressible is said, the unimaginable is described and the remedy to this crime is outlined.

In this article I would like to recall the stages that led to the adoption of the Declaration, before discussing how its interpretation since 1992 by the Working Group has allowed this document to live "with the times." Even with the adoption of the Convention and the development of international law on the issue of enforced disappearances, there are still new challenges appearing for the Declaration and for the Working Group, to which we will devote several lines.

II. TOWARDS THE ADOPTION OF THE DECLARATION

Before starting, I would like to share a few quick words on the elaboration of the Declaration. We must bear in mind that everything started in 1981, when the Human Rights Institute of the Paris Bar organized an international conference on "The Refusal to Forget" under the chairmanship of Nobel Peace Price Adolfo Pérez Esquivel, where Louis

Joinet was the General Rapporteur.[1] As Joinet himself recalls, it was in this occasion that Julio Cortázar pronounced a discourse that continues to be for us all a sort of guidance in the dark night of enforced disappearances, a categorical imperative in the fight against this practice, particularly when he evoked

> *the invisible presence of thousands of disappeared (...) in this room where they are not, where they are referred to as a topic of work (...) we must feel them present and close, sitting among us, watching us, speaking to us. The lone fact that among the participants and public attending there are the parents and friends of those disappeared makes this countless multitude even more perceptible, reunited in a silent witness, in a relentless accusation.*

But also:

> *We must maintain in this obstinate present, with all its blood and ignominy, that which we seek to bring into the comfortable country of oblivion. We must continue to consider as living those who may not be, and we have the obligation to reclaim them, one by one, until the answer finally brings forward the truth that we seek to evade today.*

Guided by this imperative, the drafting process of an international convention started with a first draft presented in 1982 by FEDEFAM, and a second one in 1988, which was adopted in a conference in Buenos Aires. On that same year, the Working Group on detention of the Sub-Commission of Human Rights seized a draft on a Declaration for the Protection of All Persons Against Enforced or Involuntary Disappearances. The initiative was proposed by several NGOs, relayed by Louis Joinet as member of the Sub-Commission: in 1990, the Working Group adopts the draft Declaration and presents it to the Sub-Commission, which also adopts it and transmits it to the Commission. The Commission created then an open-ended Working Group charged with examining the draft declaration.[2] The Working Group labored under the efficient chairmanship of the representative of France, Ms. Béatrice Le Fraper-du-Hellen, and held 20 sessions, from 28 October

1 On this and the following, see L. JOINET, "De la Déclaration de 1992 à la Convention de 2006 (chronologie de l'élaboration)" in E. DECAUX and O. DE FROUVILLE (eds.), *La Convention pour la protection de toutes les personnes contre les disparitions forcées*, Bruylant, Brussels 2009, p. 29.

2 Commission on Human Rights, *Question of enforced of involuntary disappearances*, Res. 1991/41 (5 March 1991).

to 8 November 1991, and on 20 January 1992, before adopting a draft Declaration, which was then adopted verbatim by the Commission and later by the General Assembly on 18 December 1992.[3]

It must be noted that at the time, the Declaration constituted the only international instrument dealing with the issue of enforced disappearances. The Inter-American Convention, whose drafting started in 1987, would not be adopted until 1994.

III. THE WORKING GROUP AS INTERPRETER AND GUARDIAN OF THE DECLARATION

The Working Group received with enthusiasm the adoption of the Declaration. In its 1993 report, it wrote:

> *The Working Group, which participated actively in the elaboration of this Declaration, welcomes it as a milestone in the united efforts to combat the practice of disappearance and considers that it constitutes an important basis for its own future work. Many proposals and recommendations which the Working Group has adopted over the years and published in its annual reports have been reflected in the Declaration.*[4]

Furthermore, the Working Group underlines in the same report that:

> *In its resolution 1993/35 of 5 March 1993, entitled "Question of enforced or involuntary disappearances", the Commission on Human Rights invited all Governments to take appropriate legislative or other steps to prevent and punish the practice of enforced disappearances, with special reference to the Declaration and to take action to that end nationally, regionally and in cooperation with the United Nations. In the same resolution, the Commission also requested the Working Group to take into account the provisions of the Declaration and invited it to cite in its future reports any obstacles to the proper application of the Declaration and to recommend means of overcoming them.*[5]

---

3 Commission on Human Rights, *Report of the Working Group on the Declaration on the protection of all persons from enforced disappearance*, E/CN.4/1992/19/Rev.1 (31 January 1992).

4 Commission on Human Rights, *Report of the Working Group on Enforced or Involuntary Disappearances*, E/CN.4/1994/26 (22 December 1993), par. 74.

5 *Id.*, par. 77.

As a direct consequence, the Working Group decided to send letters to all Member States of the United Nations and to NGOs, asking them to provide information on the measures taken to implement the Declaration at the national level, and on the obstacles found for its application. The census on the obstacles that were identified by NGOs was already eloquent at the time, and it is saddening to note that those obstacles are still a reality today:

> *The obstacles to the proper implementation of the Declaration cited in most of the replies from non-governmental organizations are fairly similar and may be summarized as follows:*
>
> *(a) Internal strife and armed conflicts have been cited as the major political reasons for the widespread practice of enforced disappearances;*
> *(b) In most cases there appears to be a lack of political will on the part of Governments to terminate the phenomenon of disappearances;*
> *(c) Far-reaching emergency laws and regulations lead to serious restrictions on the right to habeas corpus, to uncontrolled powers of military authorities, and to a general inefficiency of the civilian judicial system, thereby creating a climate conducive to acts of enforced disappearance;*
> *(d) Broad powers of arrest authorizing or at least tolerating the carrying out of arrests by plainclothed security personnel in unmarked vehicles who do not give reasons or identify themselves, are mentioned as a common practice leading to disappearances;*
> *(e) The allowing of incommunicado detention and the lack of central computerized registers of all detainees and of daily records of places of detention are cited as serious obstacles to an efficient implementation of the Declaration;*
> *(f) Most Governments have not enacted special laws explicitly prohibiting the practice of enforced disappearance in accordance with articles 3, 4 and 5 of the Declaration. In countries where all acts of enforced disappearance are established as offences under criminal law, these offences are often defined in such vague terms that it seems extremely difficult to prove the causal relation between arrest and disappearance;*
> *(g) The lack of impartial investigation of all cases of alleged disappearances, the lack of access of civilian investigatory agencies to all places of detention (in particular military detention centres) and the lack of sincere efforts to identify victims of disappearances are serious obstacles to tracing disappeared persons;*
> *(h) Amnesty laws, due obedience laws, statutes of limitations, presidential pardons and the lack of impartial proceedings before military courts lead to impunity for perpetrators of enforced disappearances and thereby constitute a serious obstacle to the prevention of further acts of disappearances;*

(i) *Finally, many non-governmental organizations reported that most Governments have so far failed to distribute the Declaration among their legislative, judicial and administrative authorities or to make it available to the public at large.*[6]

In its 1995 report, the Working Group noted that despite its efforts to encourage Governments to adopt measures for the application of the Declaration, little progress has been made. The Working Group underlines the fact that the obligations deriving from the Declaration are not only applicable to those States where acts of enforced disappearance have been committed. Thus, in an effort to attract the attention of States on their obligations, the Working Group decided in its 47th session to adopt two General Comments on articles 3 and 4 of the Declaration.

To summarize, the Working Group took two fundamental measures on the basis of the mandate that was entrusted to it by States regarding the Declaration. First, it made a census of the obstacles for the implementation of the Declaration. It is the basis of its current procedure of "general allegations", by virtue of which it receives allegations of enforced disappearances that are then transmitted to States to receive their comments. Then, acting upon the information and practices compiled in the census, it started to interpret and explain the provisions of the Declaration with a view to facilitate its application by States at the national level. This is the sense of general comments, which as of today are eleven in number.

Those eleven general comments did not only allow the Working Group to clarify the provisions of the Declaration, but also to make them a living instrument through an evolving interpretation, in line with the evolution of general international law. Thus, in its General Comment on enforced disappearance as a crime against humanity,[7] the Working Group considered that the contextual elements of the crime against humanity must be interpreted in light of article 7 of the Rome Statute, a faithful reflection itself of customary international law on this issue. On the contrary, the Working Group considered in its General Comment on the definition of

6 *Id.*, par. 86.

7 Report of the Working Group on Enforced or Involuntary Disappearances, *General Comment on enforced disappearance as a crime against humanity*, A/HRC/13/48 (21 December 2009), par. 39.

enforced disappearance[8] that the definition contained in the Rome Statute deviated from customary law on this issue, and argued that it was better reflected by the Convention of 2006. Another example: in its General Comment on enforced disappearance as a continuous crime,[9] the Working Group takes into consideration the evolution of national and international practice to affirm that "one consequence of the continuing character of enforced disappearance is that it is possible to convict someone for enforced disappearance on the basis of a legal instrument that was enacted after the enforced disappearance began, notwithstanding the fundamental principle of non retroactivity."[10]

These examples show that the innovative character of the Declaration was maintained and prolonged by the Working Group. As a matter of fact, the Working Group became the supervising organ of the Declaration, and it's in part for its role as an intermediary that this text continues to have an important degree of influence on international law. The question today is to know if the entry into force of the Convention and the establishment of the Committee do not call into question the role played until now by the Declaration and the Working Group.

IV. NEW CHALLENGES

To this question, it seems to me that any response must be nuanced. It is evident that the Convention has become the text of reference in international law for enforced disappearance, and particularly in relation to the Declaration. As a conventional instrument carefully elaborated and much more detailed in certain aspects than the Declaration, and which aims to set forth binding international norms, this was an expected and normal outcome. It is even desirable, since the Convention is a text that has as its purpose to become universal; the Working Group, just as all the other actors working on enforced disappearances, has taken on to

8 Report of the Working Group on Enforced or Involuntary Disappearances, *General Comment on the definition of enforced disappearance*, A/HRC/7/2 (10 January 2008), par. 26.

9 Report of the Working Group on Enforced or Involuntary Disappearances, *General Comment on enforced disappearance as a continuous crime*, A/HRC/16/48 (26 January 2011), par. 39.

10 *Id.*

realize this objective by promoting the ratification of the Convention by the largest number of States. The Working Group actively contributes to this promotional campaign of the Convention: it has never failed, in each of its bilateral meetings, to encourage States that have not yet done so to ratify the Convention, and to formulate the declarations of acceptance of jurisdiction for individual and inter-State complaints. It has been the same throughout its country visits: since 2006, the Working Group systematically recommends to States to ratify the Convention, and makes itself available to help them in an effort to facilitate ratification.

Furthermore, it seems evident that the interpretation of the Declaration is now closely linked to that of the Convention. On the one hand, it is actually imperative that similar provisions between the Declaration and the Convention are interpreted coherently. On the other hand, it is evident that the Committee will have the task of interpreting the Convention. Thus, the interpretation of the Declaration will be made in function of the interpretation made by the Committee on the clauses that are similar to those of the Convention.

This doesn't mean that the Declaration will lose its importance in this new context, or that the Working Group will be called to abandon the functions it performs in regard to the Declaration. A first consideration is that the Declaration continues to be the text of reference for those States that are not bound by another conventional instrument. Even if we would like the Convention to quickly become a universal instrument, this transitional phase will probably last for some time.

Secondly, all the normative acquis deriving from general comments of the Working Group in relation to the Declaration will have to be taken in consideration for the interpretation of the Convention. In this regard, the Declaration and the Working Group will continue to play a role, even if it's evident that this acquis will bot bind the Committee, which is "sovereign" in its interpretation of the Convention.

Finally, there is the fact that the Declaration contains provisions that the Convention does not, or that it treats certain issues from an angle that is not present in the Convention. On these issues, the Declaration will remain a source of inspiration and a reference point, both in the elaboration of international law and for the interpretation of the Convention, but also in the elaboration of national legislation. Four particular questions can be identified in this context: the issue of the risk of enforced disappearance in the decision of granting asylum (article 15 of the Declaration); the exclusion of military tribunals to try the authors of enforced disappearances (article 16, par. 2); the issue of privileges and immunities for the authors of disappearances (article 16, par. 3); and the issue of amnesties and other analogous measures (article 18, par. 1).

On all of these issues, the Declaration continues to be a text of reference that needs to be reevaluated against the evolution of customary international law on the question of enforced disappearances.

EXTREME POVERTY AND HUMAN RIGHTS

A Social Struggle Against a Global Issue

Magdalena Sepúlveda Carmona*

I. THE SPECIAL PROCEDURES OF THE UN HUMAN RIGHTS COUNCIL AND THE MANDATE OF THE SPECIAL RAPPORTEUR ON EXTREME POVERTY AND HUMAN RIGHTS

The mandate of the Special Rapporteur on extreme poverty and human rights is one of the United Nations special procedures – the mechanisms established by the Commission on Human Rights and assumed by the Human Rights Council to address either specific country situations or thematic issues in all parts of the world. Special Procedures are human rights monitoring mechanisms endorsed to individual experts called "Special Rapporteurs", "Independent Experts" or "Working Groups", whose common mandate is the investigation and reporting of human rights situations either in a specific territory (country mandates) or with regard to a phenomenon of violations (thematic mandates).

The scope of the action of special procedures is truly universal: all the States of the world are monitored by these bodies and they cover civil, political, economic, social and cultural rights. Mandate holders report on their activities and findings to the most important United Nations bodies dealing with human rights, the Human Rights Council and the General Assembly. They also carry out country visits to investigate the situation of

---

* Senior Research Fellow at the United Nations Research Institute for Social Development; former UN Special Rapporteur on extreme poverty and human rights (2008–2014). The author wishes to thank the support provided by Kate Donald and Humberto Cantú Rivera for the elaboration of this article.

human rights in specific domestic contexts. They are independent, serve in a personal capacity, and they do not receive salaries or any other financial compensation for their work.

The mandate on extreme poverty and human rights was established in 1998 by the former Commission on Human Rights, with the aim of strengthening international, regional and national efforts to reduce poverty and to alleviate the effects of poverty, by protecting and promoting human rights. I was appointed as mandate holder in May 2008, and tasked with examining the relationship between the enjoyment of human rights and extreme poverty, with a particular emphasis on vulnerable groups.

When I was appointed to the position of Special Rapporteur on extreme poverty and human rights in May 2008, the international community was in the midst of devastating global financial and economic crises, the ramifications of which continue to be felt across developing and developed countries. The effect of the crises, which pushed tens of millions of people into unemployment and poverty, will linger for generations, as will the consequences of the harsh recovery and austerity policies adopted in their aftermath. I therefore decided to address the human rights implications of responses to the crises and recovery in several reports.[1] I have also addressed the impact of the crises, examining the proliferation of laws, regulations and practices that penalize and stigmatize people living in poverty, even as poverty and homelessness rates continue to rise.[2]

The onset of the crises saw development institutions, United Nations agencies and States searching for poverty reduction strategies which would withstand and help to mitigate the impact of the crises. In this regard, there was considerable interest in and support for the implementation of social protection programmes, particularly cash transfer programmes. Although social security systems have played an integral role in many States for decades, the idea of compulsory minimum level of non-contributory social protection had only really gained traction after it became a focal policy

1 Report of the Independent Expert on the question of human rights and extreme poverty, *Human rights-based approach to recovery from the global economic and financial crises, with a focus on those living in poverty*, A/HRC/17/34 (17 March 2011).

2 Report of the Special Rapporteur on extreme poverty and human rights, *The penalization of people living in poverty*, A/66/265 (4 August 2011).

for the International Labour Organization in 2001. With the advent of the crises, which put in jeopardy the significant gains in poverty alleviation that had been achieved over the preceding decade, support for social protection expanded considerably.

Thus, I decided to orient one of the primary thematic priorities of my mandate around the human rights implications of and approach to social protection programmes. In various reports to the Human Rights Council and General Assembly,[3] I set out to elaborate and promote a human rights framework for social protection, identifying best practices and disseminating lessons learned. One of the key messages of my analysis has been that human rights obligations relate not only to the final outcome of social protection programmes, but also to the process through which such programmes are implemented. The central human rights principles of the human rights framework – equality and non-discrimination (including accessibility, acceptability, affordability and the incorporation of the gender perspective), participation, transparency and accountability – must be applied to the design, implementation, monitoring and evaluation of social protection systems.

Here I will set out some examples of what a human rights approach to cash transfer programmes is (which are an increasingly popular type of social protection programme, but of course represent just one element of what should be a more comprehensive social protection strategy),[4] and I will generally outline the spirit and transcendence of the adoption of the Guiding Principles on extreme poverty and human rights for the protection of fundamental rights. Next I will discuss what I consider to be the main

3 On *human rights and cash transfer programmes*, A/HRC/11/9 (27 March 2009); on *social protection systems and the financial and economic crisis*, A/64/279 (11 August 2009); on *social protection and old age poverty*, A/HRC/14/31 (31 March 2010); on *the importance of social protection measures in achieving the Millennium Development Goals*, with a particular focus on gender-related concerns, A/65/259 (9 August 2010); and on a *human rights-based approach to recovery from the global economic and financial crises, with a focus on those living in poverty*, A/HRC/17/34 (17 March 2011), which included an analysis of the important role played by social protection programmes during times of crisis and recovery.

4 A more complete overview can be found in M. SEPÚLVEDA and C. NYST, *The Human Rights Approach to Social Protection*, Ministry for Foreign Affairs of Finland, Helsinki 2012, available at www.ohchr.org/Documents/Issues/EPoverty/HumanRightsApproachToSocialProtection.pdf (last accessed 15 February 2015).

characteristics that social protection programmes using cash transfers must have, in order to be anchored in a solid and adequate basis that aims at the reduction and eventual eradication of poverty. It is also necessary that they have an integral perspective with a human rights-based approach, and that they take into consideration the limits that poverty imposes in the general enjoyment of human rights.

II. SOCIAL PROTECTION PROGRAMMES (CASH TRANSFER): CHARACTERISTICS AND PRINCIPLES OF A HUMAN RIGHTS-BASED APPROACH

In order for social protection programmes to be effective and fulfil their objective appropriately before the poorer strata in society, they must have certain characteristics and principles aiming at the protection of human rights. Such programs should also include elements that lead to fairness in the use and enjoyment of resources among those most in need. In the following paragraphs, I will detail some characteristics and principles that are fundamental for the success of social protection programs, using cash transfers as an example.[5]

A. CHARACTERISTICS

a. Legal and institutional framework

Cash transfer programmes have been established in the region through a wide range of legal and institutional frameworks. In some cases, cash transfer programmes are institutionalized and incorporated into a national social protection strategy, generally through domestic laws, including constitutional legislation, such as in the case of Brazil. In most cases, however, cash transfer programmes are based only on presidential decrees, policy statements or simply operational manuals and guidelines.

The establishment of a programme through adequate legal and institutional frameworks is essential in order to ensure that there is clarity regarding

---

[5] Cash transfers are only one type of social protection programmes, and should be a part of a larger social protection system.

the various roles and responsibilities of government entities involved in its operation. Moreover, this is necessary to avoid political manipulation, abuses or even the lack of certainty in relation to the duration of the programme, which has a negative impact in its beneficiaries.

Without a legal and institutional framework and a long-term strategy, beneficiaries are not in a position to claim their rights, and programmes may therefore be more prone to be used for electoral purposes. Where legal and institutional frameworks are clear and efficient, there is less risk that political changes jeopardize the existence of cash transfer programmes, which in turn protects its beneficiaries.

b. Strategy and global view of poverty alleviation

For these programmes to be effective, they need to be a part of wider national strategies to face the multi-dimensional character of poverty. States must ensure the full integration of cash transfer programmes within a wide range of social policies, as well as the existence of a sufficient and quality provision of public services, particularly in the fields of education and health coverage.

B. PRINCIPLES

a. Equality and non discrimination

The principle of equality and non discrimination demands that States adopt a series of measures to ensure equal treatment to all individuals under their jurisdiction. This principle must be at the center of the design and implementation of social protection systems undertaken by States, and should be made clear particularly throughout the pillars that support those programmes, such as those mentioned next.

1) Prioritize the most disadvantaged groups

States must ensure that targeting mechanisms and eligibility criteria are fair, effective, transparent and non-discriminatory, and give priority to the most disadvantaged and marginalized individuals and groups.

While no targeting mechanism can ever be perfect, from a human rights perspective inclusion errors (providing the benefit to someone who is not in the target group) are not as problematic as exclusion errors (failure to provide the transfer to those targeted).

Universal provision of cash transfer programmes is the simplest and most transparent structure, and with the lowest administrative costs. Universal coverage reduces the opportunities for corruption and has no stigma attached for the beneficiaries. In this sense, cash transfer programmes, as well as other social policies, should aim at ensuring universal access.

The cost of delivering universal cash transfers is often viewed as a major impediment. Nonetheless, costing studies suggest that they are affordable even in low-income countries. Therefore, the impediment appears to be more of a political nature than an economic one.

When programmes are not universal, the methods of wealth calculation used by many programmes to determine the beneficiaries require much caution. These methods require sophisticaded administration systems that may lead to exclusion errors that are discriminatory. Moreover, the more complicated the adopted method of calculation is, the more opaque the eligibility criteria becomes, which may render scrutiny of the process by beneficiaries difficult, if not impossible. In addition, as the process becomes less transparent it becomes more difficult for individuals to access the program, or to consider it as a right and not as a political sinecure.

2) Gender equality

Men and women are affected in different ways by the cash transfer programmes. A gender-based approach is required to refine the analysis on the potential impact of these programmes in the enjoyment of human rights by women living in extreme poverty.

For cash transfer programmes to contribute in reducing gender inequality, it is essential that legislative and other measures are adopted with the aim of removing the barriers that limit political participation, access to education and to other productive assets, such as land and credit, of women. Without security, power or resources, women cannot participate and claim their rights.

Some States implement the so-called conditional cash transfer programmes, also known as co-responsibility programmes. Under such programmes, the benefits are tied to the beneficiaries' commitment (mainly women heads of household) to enrolling their children in school or regularly taking their children for health check-ups. Those programmes should be analyzed with caution.

Such conditional cash transfer programmes may create an unnecessary burden on women while perpetuating traditional notions of gender roles within the family. Putting conditionalities on women is based on evidence suggesting that women's commitment to the well-being of their families is generally greater than that of men. However, this approach runs a high risk of perpetuating patriarchy instead of working to change it.

3) Respect of the principles of accesibility and adaptability

The principle of accesibility requires that outreach and information on cash transfer programmes must be specifically designed to reach groups that are particularly vulnerable or excluded. Information should employ channels that reach the poorest segments of society (for example, radio announcements, community plays) and must also overcome cultural barriers (for example by making information available in languages used by indigenous peoples).

Information is not sufficient to ensure accessibility to the programmes. Cash transfer programmes' outreach must also incorporate measures to remove any material, geographical and other impediments to access by certain groups who face particular obstacles, such as persons with disabilities, the elderly, indigenous peoples, minorities or people with HIV/AIDS. Special measures should be taken for administrators to reach beneficiaries living in remote rural areas.

b. Transparency and access to information

The direct transfer of cash to a large number of beneficiaries raises concerns about potential abuses by the programme administrators. It is essential that all cash transfer programmes have accountability mechanisms in order to avoid corruption, abuse, mismanagement and political manipulation. Transparency and access to information are essential elements of accountability.

Transparency means that beneficiaries –and the society at large- should be able to identify the roles and responsibilities of all stakeholders, at both the national and local level. There should also be transparency in regard to several componentes of the cash transfer programmes, such as targeting mechanisms, elegibility criteria, benefits, complaints mechanisms, and avenues for redress. These measures are essential to safeguard against abuse and maladministration of the programmes.

c. Accountability mechanisms

Cash transfer programmes without accountability and redress mechanisms are less likely to be understood in terms of entitlements and rights and are rather more likely to be viewed as instruments of clientelism, which can be manipulated by political actors.

Independent and effective mechanisms to monitor the administration of programmes and to collect and process complaints are essential to prevent abuses. Such mechanisms are essential in particular for the review of three key elements: qualification under the programme; the maintenance of the programme, with mechanisms to report instances of demands of inappropriate work, political support, demands for money, threats, or sexual harassment; and the supervision of payment procedures.

These mechanisms not only enhance the protection of the beneficiaries but they also contribute to impriving the efficiency of a cash transfer programme.

d. Significant and effective participation of the beneficiaries

The participation of persons living in extreme poverty in policies and programmes that affect them, and generally in public life, is essential for the protection of the rights of the poor. Therefore beneficiaries of cash transfer programmes must have the right to participate in the design, implementation and evaluation of the programmes.

From a human rights perspective, participation is not simply something desirable from the point of view of ownership and sustainability, but rather a right, and thus it must play a role in the design and implementation of such programmes. Due to the asymmetry of power between the beneficiaries of programmes and the authorities that administer them, beneficiaries are often unable to protect their rights. Without fair and effective mechanisms that enable beneficiaries to actively participate, cash transfer programmes are vulnerable to political manipulation.

The absence of participation also means that policymakers and programme administrators have no feedback from the beneficiaries, which in turn undermines the effectiveness and sustainability of the programmes. Participation also contributes to ensuring social cohesion and political support for cash transfer programmes.

III. THE GUIDING PRINCIPLES ON EXTREME POVERTY AND HUMAN RIGHTS

Another important area which the mandate has been able to contribute to is the development of international human rights law on the issue of poverty, through the Guiding Principles on Extreme Poverty and Human Rights.[6] These are a set of human rights standards adopted in September 2012 by the United Nations Human Rights Council, providing the first global policy guidelines applying States' human rights obligations to the specific situation of people living in poverty.

The Principles respond to the significant social, cultural, economic and structural obstacles that people living in poverty face, which prevent them from enjoying their rights and put them at increased risk of discrimination, stigma, violence, ill health and lack of education, further entrenching and exacerbating the cycle of poverty through successive generations.

Based on international human rights norms and standards, these Principles will serve as a practical tool for policy-makers to ensure that public policies (including poverty eradication efforts) reach the poorest members of society, recognize the obstacles that they face to enjoy their rights and respect and uphold all their rights.

---

6 Report of the Special Rapporteur on extreme poverty and human rights, *Final draft of the Guiding Principles on extreme poverty and human rights*, A/HRC/21/39 (18 July 2012).

A. THE HISTORY AND DEVELOPMENT OF THE GUIDING PRINCIPLES ON EXTREME POVERTY AND HUMAN RIGHTS

In 2001, the former United Nations Commission on Human Rights – now the Human Rights Council – stressed the need to develop a set of principles on the implementation of existing human rights norms and standards in the fight against extreme poverty. In response, the former UN Sub-Commission on the Promotion and Protection of Human Rights entrusted an ad hoc group of experts with the task of preparing the Draft Guiding Principles (DGPs) on Extreme Poverty and Human Rights. The DGPs were submitted by the Sub-Commission to the Human Rights Council at its second session in 2006.

From 2006 to 2009 the Office of the High Commissioner for Human Rights (OHCHR) led consultations on the draft guiding principles. These consultations were open to States, national human rights institutions, international organizations and civil society organizations. Specific consultations with people living in poverty in several regions of the world were also undertaken, which greatly contributed to shaping the Principles.

Following these consultations, the Human Rights Council invited me to facilitate the further progress of the DGPs by providing recommendations to assist States in improving and updating the current draft and incorporating the outcomes of the consultations. Accordingly, in September 2010 I presented a report to the Council, which detailed the rationale behind the proposals for improving the guiding principles and the basic conceptual definitions that should frame these proposals, addressed the main challenges experienced by persons living in extreme poverty that must be taken into account when preparing the principles, and presented an annotated outline of the proposal on how to improve the draft guiding principles.

In response, the Council invited the OHCHR to hold a broad consultation on the DGPs on the basis of the annotated outline that was included in my progress report. The objective of this consultation was to gain input from a broad range of actors, particularly States, development practitioners and civil society organisations, so that consensus and collective agreement could be reached about the principles. On the basis of these consultations, I submitted a final draft of the Principles to the Human Rights Council in September 2012. The HRC subsequently adopted the Principles on 27 September 2012.

It is important to note that people living in poverty themselves were directly involved in the drafting of the Guiding Principles through the efforts of the NGO International Movement ATD Fourth World (ATD). Among the consultations undertaken by the Sub-Commission, the most important ones were draft regional seminars held in Bangkok (Thailand), Pierrelaye (France), Pune (India) and Sao Paulo (Brazil) with people living in poverty, convened by ATD. After that, ATD as well as other NGOs were consulted on various drafts, playing a key role in ensuring that the voices of the poor were heard in the process. In drafting the Guiding Principles I was also able to take into account the views of people living in poverty whom I have met on my country missions as Special Rapporteur, who shared with me their experiences and ideas on a whole range of issues, ranging from discrimination to social protection to housing to livelihoods. Thus the formal and informal contributions of people living in poverty were essential in the development of these principles.

B. THE RATIONALE BEHIND THE GUIDING PRINCIPLES

People living in extreme poverty are often neglected or overlooked by politicians, service providers, policy-makers and others. Their lack of political voice, financial or social capital and their chronic social exclusion ensures that they are an almost invisible segment of the general population for the purposes of politics and policy.

While all human rights apply to all people, including people living in extreme poverty, due to the significant obstacles that they face in accessing their entitlements and enjoying their human rights – obstacles related to stigma, discrimination, financial constraints, social structures and others – it is necessary to clarify the implications of States' obligations with regard to the situation of people living in poverty. Many human rights violations affect people living in poverty more than any other group. Discrimination against the poor is widespread and widely tolerated. Poverty is a major cause of vulnerability to discrimination and other human rights violations, and moreover people living in poverty are often the victims of multiple and overlapping discrimination (for example on the basis of their ethnicity, gender or disability), increasing their disadvantage. Thus, States need guidance on how to put into practice their obligations to respect, protect and fulfil the rights of persons living in extreme poverty. The objective is to ensure that the poor are reached by public policies and are granted a voice in public life as full and respected members of society.

The Guiding Principles should foster effective implementation and compliance with existing human rights norms and principles. They should also help to address the gap between human rights standards and the actual situation of persons in extreme poverty, bearing in mind their diversity worldwide. At their core the Guiding Principles prioritize the importance of reaching out and protecting persons living in extreme poverty, as the most disadvantaged and marginalized individuals and groups in societies, but moreover empowering them to shape their lives and lift themselves free of poverty.

The Guiding Principles also provide an opportunity to add visibility and political momentum to the fight against extreme poverty, and address the difficulties States and the international community face in reaching those living in extreme poverty. They should empower those living in poverty through a human rights approach to alleviating poverty and provide an advocacy tool for all stakeholders working on poverty issues at the domestic and international level.

By adopting documents like the Guiding Principles, States are increasingly showing their acceptance that extreme poverty can be a cause or consequence of a human rights violation.

When poverty is caused, exacerbated or perpetuated by acts or omissions of the State, there is a direct link between the situation of poverty and violations to the rights included in the Universal Declaration of Human Rights, the International Covenant on Civil and Political Rights (ICCPR), the International Covenant on Economic, Social and Cultural Rights (ICESR) and other human rights instruments. For example, most obviously people living in extreme poverty do not enjoy the right to an adequate standard of living (ICESR article 11 and UDHR article 25). Often they do not enjoy the right to work or to 'just and favourable conditions at work' (ICESCR articles 6 & 7 and UDHR article 23).

However there are also many civil and political rights persons living in poverty do not enjoy: for example the right to liberty and security of the person (ICCPR article 9) as they are often very vulnerable to violence, abuse, exploitation and crime; the right to equality before the courts and tribunals (ICCPR article 14) as they often cannot afford legal aid, bail, expert witnesses etc.; freedom from interference in privacy and family life (ICCPR article 17) for example due to intrusive and arbitrary conditionalities and assessments for welfare payments; and the right and opportunity to take part in public affairs (ICCPR article 25), suffering as they do from systemic powerlessness and lack of voice. Also, and very fundamentally, people living in poverty often do not enjoy their rights to equality and non-discrimination. They are discriminated against and subject to stigma because they are poor, and this situation worsens when besides being poor, they belong to ethnic minorities, have disabilities or belong to other vulnerable groups, which are generally over-represented among people living in poverty. Discrimination on the grounds of social or economic status is a prohibited ground of discrimination under international human rights law, being implicit in the phrase 'other status' at the end of the list of protected characteristics (nationality, race, sex, religion, etc.) included in each human rights treaty.[7]

The link between human rights and poverty reduction has often been overlooked or dismissed in the past. However, a new approach to development and the fight against poverty – one based on respecting and enforcing human rights obligations and responsibilities in conformity with fundamental human rights principles – has an enormous potential to respond more efficiently to the enormous levels of inequality and poverty that persist throughout the world.

---

7 Committee on Economic, Social and Cultural Rights, *General Comment N° 20: Non-discrimination in economic, social and cultural rights*, E/C.12/GC/20 (02 July 2009), para. 34–35.

VICTIMS, COMMUNICATIONS AND THE SPECIAL PROCEDURES OF THE UN HUMAN RIGHTS COUNCIL

Catalina Rivera Díaz*

I. INTRODUCTION

When victims of human rights abuses do not have effective access to remedies in their own domestic jurisdiction, they usually turn to other instances to look for relief. Some of those instances are at the regional level, while some others are available at the universal level. One of these cases in the latter category is that provided by the Special Procedures of the Human Rights Council, either through the complaints procedure of its Advisory Committee, or through the communications procedure of the Special Rapporteurs, Independent Experts or Working Groups on the different human rights issues they work on. The communications issued by Special Procedures mandate-holders are one of their main tools to work in the monitoring of human rights compliance by Governments around the world.

In general, the communications sent by the different thematic mandates are of two types: allegation letters on the one hand, and urgent appeals on the other. In cases of violation of multiple human rights, mandate-holders may send joint communications to the respective Government, asking them to clarify the allegations made against them. In the words of Christian Tomuschat, "it has become standard practice for [thematic rapporteurs] to send 'letters of allegation' to the governments concerned, wherein they bring to their attention conduct that apparently amounts to a breach of human rights commitments, requesting clarification, and making urgent appeals to them in case 'the alleged violations are time-sensitive in terms

* First General Attorney on Human Rights for the Human Rights Commission of Nuevo Leon (Mexico), and Professor of Law for Universidad Autónoma de Nuevo León.

of involving loss of life, life-threatening situations or either imminent or ongoing damage of a very grave nature to victims'."[1]

In both cases, the communications sent by the Special Procedures mandate-holders to the corresponding Governments contain a clear explanation of the allegations without concluding the existence of a human rights violation, a reminder of the international human rights obligations applicable to the State, and several questions that would allow the UN expert to have a clear understanding on whether the human rights violation took place. The main difference lies in the time provided by the mandates to the Governments to provide their response: whereas in allegation letters the time frame for the reply by the Government is of approximately two months, in cases of urgent appeals that time frame is reduced by half.[2]

Generally, the communications procedure of the Special Procedures mandate-holders seek to raise international awareness on human rights violations, give States the opportunity to explain themselves on allegations brought against them, create a statistical registry on alleged abuses by States, allow the UN expert to offer an interpretation of the applicable international provisions, and provide an incentive for Governments to comply with their international human rights obligations.[3] However, this is not always achieved, as many Governments decide not to give proper consideration to the communication, claim the accusations as false, or simply choose to ignore the request for information by the UN expert. This is an important issue that derives directly from the voluntary and politicized nature of international human rights law practice.

This chapter will seek to offer some brief comments in the second section on how the Special Procedures communications originated in the early days of the UN Commission on Human Rights, and on how they have evolved over time. A third section will focus on the current performance on the issue of communications by the different thematic and country mandate holders from a quantitative standpoint, trying to shed some light on the

---

1 C. TOMUSCHAT, *Human Rights: Between Idealism and Realism*, 3rd ed., Oxford University Press, Oxford 2014, p. 198.

2 O. DE SCHUTTER, *International Human Rights Law*, 2nd ed., Cambridge University Press, Cambridge 2014, p. 974.

3 P. ALSTON and R. GOODMAN, *International Human Rights*, Oxford University Press, Oxford 2013, p. 732.

rate of responses and main areas of concern for the Human Rights Council and its experts. Finally, a brief fourth section will discuss the most notable characteristics of the communications procedure, which have led some commentators to consider it a quasi-jurisdictional procedure.

II. THE ORIGINS OF SPECIAL PROCEDURES COMMUNICATIONS

Since its very early stages, the United Nations started receiving complaints and requests by individuals for alleged human rights violations by Governments. This led, within a few years, to the creation of the Commission on Human Rights by the Economic and Social Council, which was in part a response to those demands, and in part the fulfillment of the mandate of the UN Charter.[4] In particular, the Commission on Human Rights considered in its first session the issue of communications on human rights, where it agreed that it would compile a confidential list of communications before each session and furnish it to its members.[5]

In 1947, the Economic and Social Council decided to go further in relation to this issue, requesting the Secretary-General to not only compile a list of communications, but also to transmit to any Member State a brief note on the substance of any communication brought against them.[6] This would become the basis for the future development of communications between UN experts and Member States. However, in that very moment, any possibility of action was completely limited, given that the Commission itself recognized that it had no power to act upon the communications received.[7]

This official position was nevertheless relative, as records of 1959 show: "… it was stated that no real improvement was possible as long as the Council continued to approve "the statement that 'the Commission recognizes that

4 S.P. SUBEDI, 'Protection of Human Rights through the Mechanism of United Nations Special Rapporteurs' (2011) 33 *HRQ (Human Rights Quarterly)* 201, 205.

5 Commission on Human Rights, *Report to the Economic and Social Council on the First Session of the Commission*, E/259 (1947), par. 21.

6 Economic and Social Council, *Resolutions adopted by the Economic and Social Council during its Fifth Session*, E/573 (02 September 1947), Res. 75(V), par. (e).

7 Commission on Human Rights, *Report to the Economic and Social Council on the First Session of the Commission*, E/259 (1947), par. 22.

it has no power to take any action in regard to any complaint concerning human rights'" and that the Committee had done all it could within these limitations."[8] In addition, an interaction between Governments and the Commission had already begun, as shown by the records of the fifteenth session in 1959, where Governments sending replies were to be asked if they wished their replies to be presented to the Commission in summary or in full.[9]

A possible motive for this view was the growing number of communications received year after year. According to the report of the eleventh session of the Commission held in 1955, the confidential list of communications kept by the Commission compiled 5,982 communications received in 1954.[10] That number would grow by the fifteenth session, held in 1959, where 6,277 communications were received only in 1958.[11] However, after 1960, no record was made public on the number of communications received by the Commission.

In 1980, the establishment of the mandate of the UN Working Group on Enforced or Involuntary Disappearances set forth what would become the bedrock for the development and use of communications in their present form. Thus, the resolution creating the Working Group determined that it should seek and receive information from different credible and reliable sources,[12] and be able to respond effectively to that information.[13] Most of the mandates established in that decade included those provisions. For example, the mandate of the Special Rapporteur on summary or arbitrary executions, established in 1982, included a provision whereby he was tasked with seeking and receiving information from different sources.[14]

---

8 Commission on Human Rights, *Report of the Fifteenth Session*, E/3229 (1959), par. 253.

9 Commission on Human Rights, *Report of the Fifteenth Session*, E/3229 (1959), Section XIV.IV, par. (f).

10 Commission on Human Rights, *Report of the Eleventh Session*, E/2731 (June 1955), par. 180.

11 Commission on Human Rights, *Report of the Fifteenth Session*, E/3229 (1959), par. 247.

12 Commission on Human Rights, *Question of missing and disappeared persons*, UN Res. 20 (XXXVI) (29 February 1980), par. 3.

13 Commission on Human Rights, *Question of missing and disappeared persons*, UN Res. 20 (XXXVI) (29 February 1980), par. 6.

14 Commission on Human Rights, *Summary or arbitrary executions*, E/RES/1982/35 (7 May 1982), par. 4.

The mandate-holder on torture and other cruel, inhuman or degrading treatment or punishment was entrusted to seek and receive information from credible sources and to respond effectively to credible and reliable information, while the resolution requested the Secretary-General to appeal to all Governments to furnish all information requested by the mandate.[15] The same provisions were included in the mandate entrusted to the Special Rapporteur on religious intolerance.[16] Thus, these mandates marked the start of a (relative) bidirectional dialogue between special procedures mandate-holders and Governments in the form of communications.

Two of the mandates adopted in the early 1990s went further in the specificity of the provisions regarding communications. In particular, the Special Rapporteur on the sale of children, child prostitution and child pornography was given a very precise mandate in this regard, when the Commission on Human Rights invited the mandate-holder to take into consideration "the need to be in a position to use any credible and reliable information made available to him, to request the Governments concerned to state their views and comment on any information he intends to include in his report and to carry out this task with discretion and independence…"[17] Yet another distinctive provision included within the mandate of other special procedure was that of the UN Working Group on Arbitrary Detention. In 1991, the Commission charged the Working Group "with the task of investigating cases of detention imposed arbitrarily or otherwise inconsistently with the relevant international standards" and to "seek and receive information from Governments and intergovernmental and non-governmental organizations"[18]

In the case of the six previously mentioned mandates, their first (and in some cases their second) reports to the Commission on Human Rights already made reference to communications interchanged with many governments. The most surprising example is that of the Working Group

15 Commission on Human Rights, *Torture and other cruel, inhuman or degrading treatment or punishment*, E/CN.4/RES/1985/33 (13 March 1985), pars. 3, 4, 6.

16 Commission on Human Rights, *Implementation of the Declaration on the Elimination of All Forms of Intolerance and of Discrimination Based on Religion or Belief*, E/CN.4/RES/1986/20, pars. 4, 5, 7.

17 Commission on Human Rights, *Sale of children*, E/CN.4/RES/1990/68 (07 March 1990), par. 3.

18 Commission on Human Rights, *Question of arbitrary detention*, E/CN.4/RES/1991/42 (05 March 1991), pars. 2–3.

on enforced or involuntary disappearances, which in its first report in 1981 mentioned that it received information regarding 11,000 to 13,000 cases of enforced disappearances in 15 countries.[19] The rest of the mandates also had varying degrees of interaction with different countries. For example, the Special Rapporteur on summary or arbitrary executions identified in his first report to the Commission in 1983, different cases of alleged summary or arbitrary executions in 39 different countries, describing in detail the allegations transmitted to the corresponding governments, and their answer (or lack thereof).[20] The Special Rapporteur on torture and other cruel, inhuman or degrading treatment or punishment detailed in his first report to the Commission in 1986 that he had identified 33 country situations, of which only 11 States responded to his correspondence seeking for clarification.[21]

In addition, the mandate-holder on religious intolerance briefly identified in his first report situations in 40 countries that were incompatible with international human rights standards,[22] and in his second report, he clearly explained the allegations transmitted to seven countries and included the four replies received.[23] In the case of the Special Rapporteur on the sale of children, he described one specific case to have allegedly taken place in the territories of Bangladesh and Pakistan.[24] Finally, the Working Group on arbitrary detention mentioned in its first report that it had issued 223 letters to 19 countries in its first nine months of work, receiving responses from eight of them.[25]

---

19 Report of the Working Group on Enforced or Involuntary Disappearances, E/CN.4/1435 (26 January 1981), pars. 44–45.

20 Report by the Special Rapporteur on summary or arbitrary executions, E/CN.4/1983/16 (31 January 1983), pars. 125–216.

21 Report by the Special Rapporteur on torture and other cruel, inhuman or degrading treatment or punishment, E/CN.4/1986/15 (19 February 1986), pars. 59–60.

22 Report by the Special Rapporteur on the implementation of the Declaration on the Elimination of All Forms of Intolerance and of Discrimination based on Religion or Belief, E/CN.4/1987/35 (24 December 1986), par. 28.

23 Report by the Special Rapporteur on the implementation of the Declaration on the Elimination of All Forms of Intolerance and of Discrimination based on Religion or Belief, E/CN.4/1988/45 (06 January 1988), pars. 15–22, 37–39.

24 Report of the Special Rapporteur on the sale of children, E/CN.4/1992/55 (22 January 1992), par. 35.

25 Report of the Working Group on Arbitrary Detention, E/CN.4/1992/20 (21 January 1992), pars. 14–22.

This clearly shows how the position held by the Commission on Human Rights in 1959 evolved, to give way to an international procedure that was becoming standardized across the different human rights mandates, and that became relatively more transparent. One important aspect to notice is the transformation of the nature of the communications procedures by mandate-holders, which seems to have happened implicitly rather than explicitly, and that is best reflected in the first report of the Working Group on arbitrary detention. Initially, all communications were considered to be completely voluntary for States, with the Commission trying to avoid a confrontational stance. However, in the definition of its methods of work, the Working Group on arbitrary detention considered that "such investigation should be of an adversarial nature so as to assist it in obtaining the cooperation of the State concerned by the case considered."[26]

While from the reports of the Commission on Human Rights it is not clear when this change of position occurred, it is possible that such a change was the result of the adoption of several binding international human rights law instruments, both at the universal and regional level, which turned many of those rights into international legal obligations. This situation potentially made the Commission aware of the evolving status of international human rights law, and of the slow erosion of the sovereignty veil held by most States as a shield from international oversight.[27] It is particularly interesting how many of these early mandates, which dealt with some of the most abhorrent violations to human rights,[28] began to build a general platform from which the special procedures would develop, and which would later on translate to other mandates (including those on economic, social and cultural rights) that were adopted in the late 1990s.

Most thematic mandates adopted in the 1990s and early 2000s included provisions on communications. In the field of civil and political rights, for example, the mandates on the right to freedom of expression,[29]

---

26 Report of the Working Group on Arbitrary Detention, E/CN.4/1992/20 (21 January 1992), par. 13.

27 S.P. SUBEDI, above n 4, at 202.

28 H. HANNUM, 'Reforming the Special Procedures and Mechanisms of the Commission on Human Rights' 7 *HRLR (Human Rights Law Review)* 73, 84, where the author explains that some mandates respond on a humanitarian basis to allegations of human rights violations.

29 Commission on Human Rights, *Right to freedom of opinion and expression*, E/CN.4/RES/1993/45 (5 March 1993), pars. 12–15.

contemporary forms of racism,[30] violence against women,[31] independence of judges and lawyers,[32] migrants,[33] and human rights defenders[34] all included provisions requesting the mandate-holders to gather, seek, receive and examine information from reliable and credible sources on alleged human rights violations corresponding to their mandates, and to respond to them effectively. In addition, the resolutions requested Governments to cooperate fully with the mandates, including by furnishing all requested information and by reacting promptly to urgent appeals sent by the mandates. The same approach was undertaken in the field of economic, social and cultural rights, where the resolutions establishing the mandates on the right to education,[35] food,[36] adequate housing,[37] and health[38] contained provisions asking the mandate-holders to seek, receive, take into consideration and respond

30 Commission on Human Rights, *Measures to combat contemporary forms of racism, racial discrimination, xenophobia and related intolerance*, E/CN.4/RES/1993/20 (2 March 1993); see also Report by the Special Rapporteur on contemporary forms of racism, racial discrimination, xenophobia and related intolerance, E/CN.4/1994/66 (2 February 1994), par. 38, for the methods of work of the mandate, which explicitly included communications on alleged violations.

31 Commission on Human Rights, *Question of integrating the rights of women into the human rights mechanisms of the United Nations and the elimination of violence against women*, E/CN.4/RES/1994/45 (04 March 1994), pars. 7(a), 9.

32 Commission on Human Rights, *Independence and impartiality of the judiciary, jurors and assessors and the independence of lawyers*, E/CN.4/RES/1994/41 (4 March 1994), pars. 3(a), 4.

33 Commission on Human Rights, *Human rights of migrants*, E/CN.4/RES/1999/44 (27 April 1999), pars. 3(a), 5, 8.

34 Commission on Human Rights, *Human rights defenders*, E/CN.4/RES/2000/61 (26 April 2000), pars. 3(a), 4.

35 Commission on Human Rights, *Question of the realization in all countries of the economic, social and cultural rights contained in the Universal Declaration of Human Rights and in the International Covenant on Economic, Social and Cultural Rights, and study of special problems which the developing countries face in their efforts to achieve these human rights*, E/CN.4/RES/1998/33 (17 April 1998), par. 6(a)(i).

36 Commission on Human Rights, *The right to food*, E/CN.4/RES/2000/10 (17 April 2000), pars. 11(a), 14.

37 Commission on Human Rights, *Question of the realization in all countries of the economic, social and cultural rights contained in the Universal Declaration of Human Rights and in the International Covenant on Economic, Social and Cultural Rights, and study of special problems which the developing countries face in their efforts to achieve these human rights*, E/CN.4/RES/2000/9 (17 April 2000), par. 7(d)(i).

38 Commission on Human Rights, *The right of everyone to the enjoyment of the highest attainable standards of physical and metal health*, E/CN.4/RES/2002/31 (22 April 2002), pars. 5(a), 10.

to information from all relevant sources. Even other multidimensional mandates, such as those on the rights of indigenous peoples[39] or on the effect of toxic waste[40] on human rights established that the experts should gather, investigate, monitor, examine, exchange and receive information related to their mandate, and urged Governments to cooperate fully by providing information or responding promptly to urgent appeals.

The standardization of the communications procedure by most mandates established by the Commission on Human Rights, and later on by the Human Rights Council, gives the impression that a set of quasi-jurisdictional universal procedures were established. This tool has certainly become another avenue for people whose human rights have been injured to ask for international oversight on the actions or omissions of a given State. However, as the figures that will be reviewed in the next section of this chapter indicate, some issues continue to demand a higher degree of attention from Governments, given the amount of communications sent by the mandates in recent years.

III. CURRENT PRACTICE OF SPECIAL PROCEDURES MANDATE-HOLDERS REGARDING COMMUNICATIONS

The general practices and methods of work of Special Procedures have not particularly changed since their inception in 1980. However, their multiplication has brought an enhanced oversight on the actions and omissions of States at the domestic level. This has translated into a continuously increasing demand for communications with the intent of safeguarding and protecting the rights of individuals or groups in danger, or of ensuring the provision of appropriate remedies. An analysis of those communications, and particularly of the remedies offered from a qualitative standpoint, is beyond the scope of this article. However, a quantitative analysis can offer a clear glimpse into the protective aspect of the work of Special Procedures mandate-holders, especially on the number of communications sent and of replies received.

---

39 Commission on Human Rights, *Human rights and indigenous issues*, E/CN.4/RES/2001/57 (24 April 2001), pars. 1(a), 7.

40 Commission on Human Rights, *Adverse effects of the illicit movement and dumping of toxic and dangerous products and wastes on the enjoyment of human rights*, E/CN.4/RES/1995/81 (8 March 1995), pars. 7(b), 11.

The most recent communications report[41] presented by Special Procedures mandate-holders to the Human Rights Council show that the level of efficacy of this procedure still has room for improvement, but also serves to highlight which issues are more pressing in the human rights field. For example, a first look at the big picture shows that slightly more than half of the communications sent to States by the different mandate-holders have been replied to, in the period between June 2006 (with the start of the work of the Human Rights Council) and 31 January 2015. Most of them have originated in thematic mandates, with approximately two percent of them being issued for by country mandate-holders. Thus, 14,346 communications have been issued since the Human Rights Council started functioning, to which 7,582 replies have been received, amounting to 52.82 percent of effectiveness from a quantitative standpoint.

Out of those 14,346 communications issued, only 281 have originated in country mandates, with the remaining 14,065 proceeding from thematic mandates. While the average level of effectiveness in communications issued by thematic procedures remains close to the overall average of the total of communications, there is an important reduction in relation to country mandates:

Thematic Mandates			
	Communications sent	Replies received	Rate of response
1 June 2006–31 January 2015	14,065	7,484	53.21%

Country Mandates[42]			
	Communications sent	Replies received	Rate of response
1 June 2006–31 January 2015	281	98	34.87%

---

41 Human Rights Council, *Communications report of Special Procedures*, A/HRC/28/85 (19 February 2015), pp. 7–8.

42 According to the latest communications report, no replies have been received from the Governments of Burundi, Eritrea and Liberia.

More telling, however, is the 'top ten' ranking of thematic mandates with most communications issued. While the UN Working Group on enforced or involuntary disappearances and the UN Working Group on arbitrary detention each has its own investigation procedures, which are not reflected in the ranking, the number of allegation letters and urgent appeals issued through the general procedures allow to have a clear notion of which human rights issues are more prevalent worldwide. This ranking is shown in the following chart:[43]

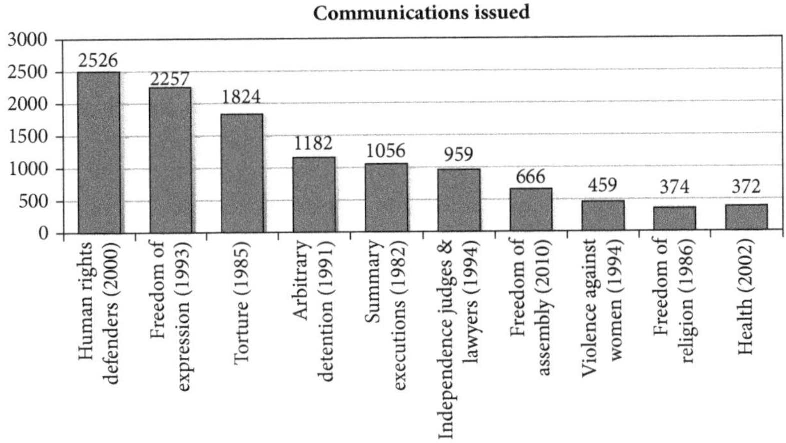

The total amount of communications issued by the above-mentioned ten Special Procedures is of 11,675, or approximately 81 percent of the total number of communications issued since 2006. Only 6,245 of them have received replies, for a response rate of approximately 53.5 percent. Of note is the fact that out of this top ten ranking, only one mandate on economic, social or cultural rights is represented. While it would be tempting to affirm that this may be due to the fact that the mandate on the right to health only originated in 2002, while the rest of the mandates represented in the chart were established in the 1980s or 1990s, the mandate on freedom of assembly could prove otherwise, given that it was only established in 2010 but has already issued more communications.

43 The chart explains the year in which each of the reflected mandates was created, and the total number of communications issued since its creation.

Most of the communications issued have dealt with the protection of human rights defenders, to which are very closely associated the mandates on freedom of expression and freedom of assembly. The mandates on torture, arbitrary detention and extrajudicial, summary or arbitrary executions, three of the most gruesome violations of international human rights law, and especially of civil and political rights, are also among the top five mandates with most communications issued. This demonstrates that prevention of these violations continues to be, at the start of the 21st century, one of the most important challenges to international human rights law.

The mandates related to economic, social and cultural rights, while having issued less communications than their counterparts on civil and political rights, could also provide a glimpse on which rights are more frequently claimed through these procedures. Until the end of January 2015, date of the last available report on communications, there has been a total of one thousand communications issued on questions related to economic, social and cultural rights, which are disaggregated in the following chart:

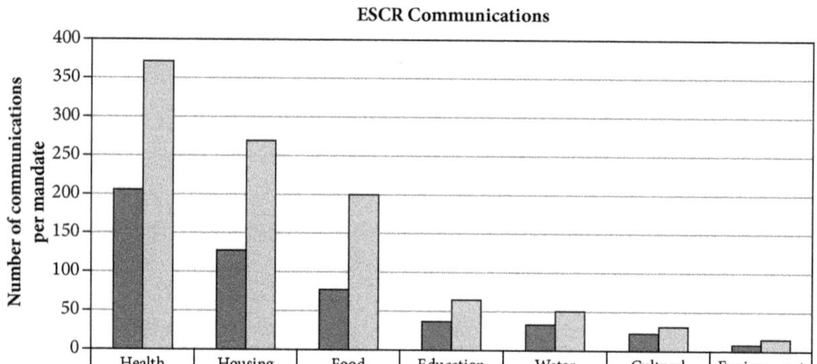

	Health (2002)	Housing (2000)	Food (2000)	Education (1998)	Water (2008)	Cultural Rights (2009)	Environment (2012)
Replied to	206	128	77	37	32	21	7
Sent	372	269	202	63	52	31	11

Of all the communications issued by the mandates on economic, social and cultural rights since their creation in the late 1990s, 508 responses have been provided, for an approximate response rate of 51 percent. In this regard, the issues most pressing in the field of economic, social and cultural rights (or in relation to which more claims have been presented before the Special Procedures) are those related to the rights to health, housing and food, which originated around the year 2000. A 'second wave' of mandates on economic, social and cultural rights took place around the end of the first and the beginning of the second decades of the 21st century, when the mandates on the right to safe drinking water and sanitation, on cultural rights and on human rights and the environment were instituted. However, very few communications related to these rights have been issued thus far.

In general, these figures demonstrate that the existence of an international set of 'procedures' has not necessarily meant that Governments are being more responsive to allegations of human rights violations, or that the Special Procedures have translated into a more effective method to protect human rights. This is likely the result of an intrinsic characteristic of any international procedure: its reliance on the effective and good-natured collaboration of the State to ensure the realization of human rights. While no other option is available at the international level than relying on the collaboration of States,[44] this doesn't exclude the fact that their non-compliance with their international commitments is a breach of international human rights law, and of their duties to uphold the highest standards in the promotion and protection of human rights and to fully cooperate with the Human Rights Council, as provided for in the UN General Assembly resolution establishing this body.[45] Thus, their lack of cooperation and work with the Special Procedures mandate-holders on the issue of communications is in itself an attempt against the work undertaken by the Human Rights Council.

One of the most accurate criticisms to the work undertaken by Special Procedures, and particularly by thematic mandates, is the lack of an effective follow-up mechanism for the communications issued by mandate-holders. The same problem can be found in relation to country visits and the recommendations issued by thematic rapporteurs therein, where few examples exist of follow-up missions. Surya Subedi has commented on this from a particularly interesting position, given her current work as Special Rapporteur on the situation of human rights in Cambodia, where she has

44 S.P. SUBEDI, above n 4, at 224, arguing that a lack of cooperation from Governments renders the work of Special Procedures mandate-holders helpless, given the lack of teeth of the mechanisms to ensure cooperation.

45 General Assembly, *Human Rights Council*, A/RES/60/251 (15 March 2006), par. 9.

found that one of the major weaknesses of the system is the absence of an effective follow-up procedure to all the work undertaken by mandate-holders on questions not related to standard-setting.[46]

However, given the absence of an enforcement mechanism that ensures the collaboration of Member States with the work undertaken by Special Rapporteurs, the only option that may be available is to include in a later review of the work of the Human Rights Council a more detailed provision whereby States seeking to become Members to this body make a commitment to work closely with mandate-holders in the consideration, implementation and response to communications, reports and recommendations. In addition, consideration should be given to the possibility of national human rights institutions providing assistance in the follow-up to the actions and measures undertaken by Human Rights Council mandate-holders, given their familiarity with their corresponding Government and their permanent focus on human rights issues within their country of origin. Few measures can be adopted that can be effective against the political nature of international intergovernmental bodies;[47] however, collaborating with the existing mechanisms at the domestic level and ensuring that membership depends on sustained commitment and collaboration with the Human Rights Council and its mechanisms may be a positive step in the right direction.

IV. COMMUNICATIONS AS A QUASI-JURISDICTIONAL PROCEDURE AND OTHER CHARACTERISTICS

The use of communications by Special Procedures mandate-holders of the former Commission on Human Rights, now Human Rights Council, was not initially conceived as a quasi-jurisdictional procedure. Instead, as documents pertaining to the decades going from 1940 until the late 1960s show, they were used basically with a statistical purpose. However, with

---

46 S.P. SUBEDI, above n 4, at 216.

47 On this question, see generally D. DIENE, 'Le rôle des rapporteurs thématiques' in E. DECAUX (dir.), *Les Nations Unies et les droits de l'homme: Enjeux et défis d'une reforme*, Pedone, Paris 2006, pp. 217–221; see also R. FREEDMAN, *The United Nations Human Rights Council: A Critique and Early Assessment*, Routledge, Oxfordshire 2013, pp. 141–144.

the establishment of the UN Working Group on enforced or involuntary disappearances and other mandates, who had as their purpose to act on the communications they received, the procedures began a slow process of transformation and consolidation into a quasi-jurisdictional procedure. As I've discussed before, this process saw the procedures go from being surrounded by a veil of secrecy into a group of translucent mechanisms that provide a relatively clearer picture of how Governments address human rights issues and complaints. Thus, in addition to the claims brought before UN Treaty Bodies and the Working Group on communications of the Advisory Committee to the Human Rights Council, communications presented to the different Special Procedures are a part of the international monitoring machinery in the field of human rights.

It is considered that the work undertaken by Special Procedures mandate-holders is particularly vibrant, and that due to their work in issuing non-binding recommendations to States on human rights issues, they are "a special UN mechanism of a quasi-judicial nature."[48] However, for other bodies such as the Human Rights Committee, the activities of Special Procedures mandates are not generally considered to be "procedures of international investigation or settlement."[49] This is due particularly because of the non-conclusive character of the communications sent to and sometimes replied to by States; that is, because they generally don't determine the existence of a human rights violation, in stark contrast with the activities of individual petitions presented to UN Treaty Bodies.[50]

The debate around the quasi-jurisdictional character (or lack thereof) of Special Procedures mandates is nevertheless unnecessary to address here, in light of some other characteristics pertaining to these procedures that would be more useful and enlightening to discuss.[51] One such characteristic is the flexibility of the communications procedure of the

48 S.P. SUBEDI, above n 4, at 203.

49 N. RODLEY, 'United Nations Human Rights Treaty Bodies and Special Procedures of the Commission on Human Rights – Complementarity or Competition?' (2003) 25 *HRQ* 882, 896.

50 *Ibid.*, at 895–896, 907.

51 However, *cfr.* O. DE SCHUTTER, above n 2, at 974, where he writes that "the communications procedure is not a quasi-judicial procedure, rather it is a means to provide immediate protection to the victims, by drawing the attention of the government to certain situations."

mandates of the Human Rights Council.[52] In contrast with most other international human rights procedures, for example, complaints received by Special Procedures mandate-holders do not generally require that domestic remedies have been exhausted first before sending a communication to the concerned State. Instead, what is generally required is that the victim or its representatives give a clear description of their identity, the identity of the alleged perpetrators and any other participant in the violation, and a clear description of the facts of a violation that has occurred, that is ongoing or that is likely to occur. This may present an opportunity for the State to create a space for dialogue between the complainant, the mandate-holder and the Government, and thus open a way to resolve any controversy that may affect the human rights of an individual or group in an amicable way.

There is also no explicit rule on confidentiality for these procedures, and thus such feature will only be exercised at the discretion of the mandate-holder. Some cases may be more sensitive than others, such as those related to torture, human rights defenders, arbitrary detention or summary executions, and would therefore require a higher degree of confidentiality. In general, the names of the alleged victims or their representatives are kept from the Governments, to protect them from reprisals or retaliation.[53] Nevertheless, the substance of other mandates may present lesser risks than some of the mandates dealing with basic civil rights. Therefore, mandate-holders may opt to issue a press release if she or he considers that it may help the cause of a communication to a State, or decide not to make public any information on a specific communication until it is published in the corresponding communications report.

Another important advantage that these procedures present is that the communications that are sent (and especially urgent appeals) can be processed – or at least are expected to be processed – relatively faster than under a regular domestic procedure, and can thus get the attention of higher-level officials within the Government. This method usually requires the State to present information and adopt protective measures as soon as possible after receiving the request for information, in order to prevent a human rights violation from happening. In the words of Sir Nigel Rodley of the Human Rights Committee, "The purpose of the special procedures'

---

52 N. RODLEY, above n 49, at 897–898.

53 O. DE SCHUTTER, above n 2, at 974.

[communications] is to prevent, inhibit or stop any feared violations... a key aspect for the special procedures is to seek to have some effect and give some guidance in a short time frame..."[54]

While flexible and quick in relation to other domestic or international procedures, the communications issued by a Special Procedure face the uncertainty of the willingness of the corresponding Government to reply, on the one hand, and to adopt effective measures to protect the rights of the alleged victims, on the other hand. The existing focus and actual effect of such communications, particularly centered on 'naming and shaming' the corresponding Governments through the communications reports, may be enough to mobilize actions at the domestic level that ensure the protection of the complainants. However, they are a far cry from the legal certainty provided by other procedures, including some international ones that also rely on the cooperation of the State concerned, such as the individual petition system before UN Treaty Bodies.

Even then, the work undertaken by mandate-holders of the Human Rights Council may provide a glimmer of hope to those individuals or groups that have no effective recourse within their national jurisdiction, or who fail to obtain a protective interim measure because of their States' lack of commitment and adherence to international human rights standards, including those of a regional nature. The fact that thematic Special Procedures are not formally bound by political frontiers or decisions is the difference that makes the communications procedure special, and thus can potentially make a difference between a human rights violation and its prevention.

V. FINAL COMMENTS

The work undertaken by Special Procedures mandate-holders has been, despite the resistance from Governments, an important task in the global effort to monitor compliance with international human rights standards. In this regard, one of the most important developments has been that of communications, which through allegation letters or urgent appeals, have been important to provide another layer of protection to human rights

54 N. RODLEY, above n 49, at 907.

to those individuals or groups in danger. While statistics show that these procedures have only been effective in half of all the cases submitted to the mandate-holders attention (at least since the establishment of the Human Rights Council), the adoption of protective measures and the possibility to ensure that the human rights of individuals and groups are respected is in itself a success that cannot be easily replicated at the international level.

Despite the many challenges to their work, Special Procedures mandate-holders are in many cases the only alternative to provide effective monitoring on the implementation of human rights standards worldwide. Thus, even with the reticence and limits imposed upon them by some States, they must continue to be, in the words of Kofi Annan, former Secretary-General of the United Nations, "the "crown jewel" of the UN human rights machinery and "an essential element" in the efforts by the United Nations to protect human rights."[55]

[55] S. SUBEDI, above n 4, at 203.

NATIONAL HUMAN RIGHTS INSTITUTIONS AND THEIR COLLABORATION WITH THE SPECIAL PROCEDURES OF THE HUMAN RIGHTS COUNCIL

Minerva MARTÍNEZ GARZA*

I. INTRODUCTION

National human rights institutions (NHRIs) are the bodies in charge of protecting and promoting international human rights law at the domestic level. By acting as a counterweight and monitoring body of the powers of the State, NHRIs face important challenges, having the mission of ensuring that people within their jurisdiction live a life in dignity. This, of course, is not an easy task; the obstacles are many and very different, including political, legal, budgetary and human resources issues. Fortunately, this has not been an absolute impediment for NHRIs to perform their functions in the aim of providing citizens with alternatives to claim before the State the respect of human rights.

Even though the work of NHRIs was mostly performed at the domestic level for several years, they've progressively had a more important presence in the international arena. Since their 'regulation' with the adoption of the Paris Principles at the United Nations, their role has grown constantly. They now occupy an important place under international human rights law,[1]

---

* President of the Human Rights Commission of Nuevo Leon (Mexico).

1 According to Carver, NHRIs (should) apply international standards in their monitoring and complaint-handling functions, work as auditors of national legislation to ensure its compliance and respect of international law, and have gradually become involved in the presentation of independent reports before UN Treaty Bodies, which represents an important transformation in their functions that has taken place during the last 15 years. See R. CARVER, 'A New Answer to an Old Question: National Human Rights Institutions and the Domestication of International Law' (2010) 10:1 *HRLR (Human Rights Law Review)* 1.

sharing the stage with States, NGOs, intergovernmental bodies and regional courts, in addition to their work and presence in their own jurisdictions.

This chapter seeks to analyze succinctly the functions and commitments that national human rights institutions have at the domestic level, as well as the guidelines established by the extinct UN Commission on Human Rights to 'standardize' their performance and include them in the international landscape. From a different standpoint, we must highlight the role of NHRIs in relation to different legal orders, where they play a role as a focal point between domestic law and international law, and between the government and its population. Finally, this chapter will look into the development of NHRIs at the domestic level, and particularly the NHRI system in Mexico, pointing out to some of the measures that may help these institutions to have a closer interaction to the role assigned to them at the international level, as well as a more effective and synchronized performance in the fulfillment of their duties.

II. NHRIs UNDER INTERNATIONAL LAW: THE PARIS PRINCIPLES

National human rights institutions were 'codified' at the international level, granting them a particular status under the Annex to resolution A/RES/48/134 of the UN General Assembly, adopted on 20 December 1993.[2] With this Annex, formally called *Principles relating to the status of national institutions* and commonly referred to as the "Paris Principles", the UN General Assembly determined to establish the competence, general attributions, guarantees of independence and pluralism, working methods and the quasi-jurisdictional competence that these institutions should have. They are the result of a reunion called by the United Nations in the French capital in 1991, where the characteristics of existing NHRIs were reviewed in order to set forth universal normative standards regarding their role, composition and function.[3]

---

[2] General Assembly, *National institutions for the promotion and protection of human rights*, A/RES/48/134 (4 March 1994).

[3] P. ALSTON and R. GOODMAN, *International Human Rights*, 2nd ed., Oxford University Press, Oxford 2013, p. 1077.

NHRIs are domestic bodies with a constitutional or legislative mandate to protect and promote human rights that frequently work as the liaison mechanism between international human rights standards and the State.[4] Resolution 48/134 explicitly sets forth that their competence lies in the sphere of the promotion and protection of human rights, while also establishing their general attributions and the scope of their mandate.[5]

There are four types of attributions or functions entrusted upon them by that resolution:

A) *Analysis*: NHRIs have the responsibility to issue opinions, recommendations, proposals and reports on issues related to human rights, particularly in the following spheres:
   a. Legislative and administrative provisions, as well as those related to the organization of the judiciary, in the aim of broadening or preserving the protection of human rights;
   b. Human rights violations;
   c. Preparation of general or special reports on human rights issues;
   d. Issuing recommendations to the government for human rights violations, as well as opinions on its position and reactions.

B) *Liaison*: NHRIs have to promote the harmonization of domestic law with international standards and its effectiveness, and encourage ratification or accession of the State to international human rights instruments.

C) *International Cooperation*: within their attributions and responsibilities, NHRIs must cooperate with United Nations bodies and other regional human rights mechanisms, and contribute to the elaboration of State reports to be presented before international or regional bodies.

D) *Promotion*: one of the most important tasks entrusted to NHRIs is the promotion and education on human rights; resolution 48/134 sets forth that there must be a collaborative approach in the elaboration of

---

4 OHCHR, *National Human Rights Institutions: History, Principles, Roles and Responsibilities*, UN Publications, Geneva 2010, p. 15.

5 See also A. McBETH, J. NOLAN and S. RICE, *The International Law of Human Rights*, Oxford University Press, Melbourne 2011, p. 322.

programs related to human rights education and research, as well as public awareness activities on human rights and non-discrimination.[6]

On the one hand, the General Assembly resolution determined the composition of NHRIs and the guarantees that need to exist to ensure their independence and pluralism. To ensure a plural composition, representation of the different sectors of society must converge, including NGOs, academics, parliamentarians and government. On the other hand, to ensure the independence of NHRIs, the only existing link between the institution and the Government must be of a budgetary nature, so that it can be impartial and have absolute discretion on its decisions and actions.

Despite this, compliance with the Paris Principles is not enough to ensure the effectiveness or independence of national human rights institutions,[7] given that they must be completely neutral and objective, and not lean towards the official position of the government in turn, or on the contrary, to the position of non-governmental organizations and civil society that they may collaborate with. As it is frequently the case in the field of human rights, compliance on paper does not necessarily mean compliance in practice. Therefore, it is necessary to measure in an efficient and realistic manner the effectiveness of national human rights institutions in the fulfillment of their mandate, particularly if they wish to comply with the expectations set forth by resolution 48/134 and be an influential actor in the promotion and protection of human rights.

NHRIs currently have a double role regarding international law that extends not only to monitoring its application, as it was the case before, but to directly collaborate in it. Thus, having a much more active role and a renowned position, their duties and responsibilities go far beyond what was foreseen by the Paris Principles when they were adopted in 1993.

---

6 Some of the challenges related to the promotion of human rights as a means to prevent their violation, one of the task entrusted to NHRIs, were already identified in 1998. See M. ROCCATTI VELÁSQUEZ, 'Comisión Nacional de Derechos Humanos: Reflexiones acerca de su función, retos y perspectivas' (1998) 97 *Revista de Administración Pública* 109, 129.

7 See R. MURRAY, 'The Role of National Human Rights Institutions' in M.A. BADERIN and M. SSENYONJO (eds.), *International Human Rights Law: Six Decades after the UDHR and Beyond*, Ashgate, Surrey 2010, pp. 306–307.

III. THE INTERACTION BETWEEN INTERNATIONAL HUMAN RIGHTS LAW, DOMESTIC LAW AND NHRIs

Since 1993, national human rights institutions have had as one of their main responsibilities to function as a link between international standards and domestic law. As it was previously mentioned, they have a liaison and harmonization function between both legal orders, with the purpose of ensuring that the standardization of the latter with the first has actual effects and a real application in the corresponding national context.

Of course, the application of international law in the domestic legal regime is not limited to the monitoring of national legislation against the normative content of international treaties to which the State is a party of, nor to encouraging the State to ratify certain international treaties. Such focus would lead to a limited perspective in relation to the effectiveness of international human rights law. Quite to the opposite, as in other legal areas, whenever a specific norm is applied, it adapts to the reality before it, thus giving birth to a legal interpretation based on facts that can eventually lead to a normative development from a pragmatic or jurisprudential perspective (or quasi-jurisprudential, in the case of NHRIs that have that competence).

This allows for the establishment of criteria and guidelines in the field of human rights, which may contribute to the development, interpretation and understanding of the legal framework, and eventually to the creation of legal customs after repeated use. If this may perhaps not lead to the appearance of customary norms, it can certainly create a criterion of legal interpretation that guides the functioning and implementation of international human rights law in the domestic legal order, and that contributes to the development of a legal culture in this important branch of public international law. From this standpoint, one of the most important actions to be undertaken by national human rights institutions (where international law, domestic law and the role of these independent public bodies converge) is precisely in the real and effective implementation of the entire *corpus juris* of international human rights law. This of course does not only refer to the norms deriving from treaties, but also to the authoritative interpretation made by the different international bodies and the use of case law issued by international judicial bodies in the field of human rights.

The fusion between norms, interpretation and case law and their analysis in light of the domestic law of a given State may help that State to adapt its legal order to comply with international standards. It may also help it to undertake a self-assessment of its activity *vis-à-vis* the criteria imposed by the international community, which may allow it to adapt its functioning in a way that basic human rights prerogatives are respected.[8]

Moreover, besides its known function as a link between international and domestic legal orders, NHRIs also have the specific task of collaborating with international organizations, particularly those working in the field of human rights. The recognition made by the UN General Assembly in 1993 started a process of international legitimization that saw NHRIs have a much more active role in human rights practice worldwide.

As Murray explains, NHRIs currently hold an important position next to States, NGOs and other international bodies in the elaboration of treaties and resolutions, as well as before intergovernmental bodies and regional human rights courts.[9] Furthermore, their participation in the renovated Universal Periodic Review of the UN Human Rights Council – where they have an active role and voice immediately after the examination of the State under review –, the fact that the two treaties adopted in the 21st century have given an unprecedented role to NHRIs regarding the monitoring and implementation of the obligations contained therein,[10] and the growing participation and use of the work and reports of NHRIs by UN Treaty Bodies are a testimony to the advancement of their integration and recognition at the international level.[11]

By having that international participation, NHRIs are the best-suited vehicles to monitor, provide advice and collaborate in the implementation

---

8 As Alston and Goodman recall, by working in the borderline between domestic and international law, NHRIs can contribute to the reception of global human rights norms in the domestic legal and cultural frameworks; see P. ALSTON and R. GOODMAN, above n 3, at 1078.

9 R. MURRAY, above n 7, at 305.

10 "These new instruments move beyond the simple recognition of the existence of such bodies… to requiring them to carry out certain tasks as set out in the provisions of the instrument itself." *Id.*, at 312.

11 R. GOODMAN and T. PEGRAM, 'National Human rights Institutions, State Conformity, and Social Change' in R. GOODMAN and T. PEGRAM (eds.), *Human Rights, State Compliance, and Social Change: Assessing National Human Rights Institutions*, Cambridge University Press, Cambridge 2012, p. 2.

of international human rights law at the domestic level, provided that they have the tools, experience and sufficient capacity to efficiently transmit to States the most effective way to implement and comply with their international obligations.

Regarding the collaboration with the Special Procedures of the UN Human Rights Council, their role is far more limited than in relation to Treaty Bodies or the Universal Periodic Review, given that there are no specific procedures for them to file reports.[12] Nevertheless, their collaboration in the country visits undertaken by Special Rapporteurs, Independent Experts of Working Groups of the Human Rights Council is transcendent, for they can provide a real overview of the 'translation' of international human rights law in the domestic sphere, and on the obstacles facing its implementation and promotion. These are relevant aspects that contribute to the work of the UN experts, so that they can highlight what they consider as necessary adjustments and measures that the State must adopt to comply with its duties and commitments.[13]

IV. BROADENING THE ROLE OF NHRIs UNDER DOMESTIC LAW: PERSPECTIVES FOR MEXICO

Mexico has a broad system of public human rights bodies. In accordance with the mandate set forth in article 102-B of the Constitution, there is a National Human Rights Commission and a public body for the protection

12 Regarding the complaints filed before Special Procedures for alleged human rights violations, these are generally undertaken by NGOs or other type of institutions, and rarely by NHRIs. However, the reports presented before Treaty Bodies generally do include inputs from NHRIs. For example, in the last review of Mexico before the Committee Against Torture, seven state human rights commissions filed a report on the issue of torture within their jurisdiction, including topics such as unlawful detention, the constitutional reform on human rights, the codification of the prohibition of torture in national legislation, the results of the recommendations issued and their requests to the Committee. This document is available at www2.ohchr.org/english/bodies/cat/docs/ngos/NHRIs_Joint_Mexico_CAT49.pdf (last accessed on 30 January 2015).

13 For Hampson, the issue of cooperation with UN mechanisms must be addressed generally within the organization; he considers that in addition to involving NHRIs in the work of the mechanism, it may be useful to have their presence and collaboration in the annual meetings held by Treaty Bodies and Special Procedures mandate holders. See F.J. HAMPSON, 'An Overview of the Reform of the UN Human Rights Machinery' (2007) 7:1 *HRLR* 7, 22–23.

and promotion of human rights in each of the federal states of the country. In sum, they constitute the National Human Rights System, and given their wide number, there is a relatively sufficient infrastructure that may work efficiently to perform the functions contained in resolution 48/134 of the UN General Assembly.

Human rights commissions in Mexico have the power to hear complaints for acts or omissions of the authorities –with the exception of the Judiciary and electoral bodies-, and after their analysis, to issue public non-binding recommendations to authorities of the three levels of government for acts considered to violate human rights. The National Human Rights Commission has a general competence for cases involving federal authorities, and with some exceptions, for state or municipal authorities. The State Human Rights Commissions thus have competence for all matters taking place in their jurisdiction where state or municipal authorities are involved. Regarding the procedure, whenever an authority receives a recommendation, it has a constitutional duty to notify its acceptance or rejection. In case of default or whenever it refuses to accept the recommendation partially or in full, the authority has the obligation to explain its motives and appear before the Senate or the local legislative body.

The role played by human rights commissions in Mexico has broadened considerably since the constitutional reform on human rights of 2011, by granting constitutional status to human rights treaties ratified by the State. The reform facilitated the interaction between the international and domestic legal orders, by explicitly establishing that human rights contained in international instruments are binding for the State, which in turn widened the spectrum of protection to fully include the parameters identified by international law. However, in many cases human rights commissions fail to uphold the values and duties they were entrusted to protect.

There are several aspects whose modification could enhance the role played by these public bodies, given that their focus has largely revolved around violations to the rule of law and legal certainty, and to recommending the start of liability procedures. Even if these recommendations are important, they usually put aside the substantive content of human rights, adopting a stance of minimalist protection.[14]

---

14 A more precise critique on this can be found in H.F. CANTÚ RIVERA, 'La protección jurisdiccional de los derechos humanos internacionales en México'

Different forums have called for the transformation of the character of the recommendations issued by human rights commissions, requesting that they become mandatory. However, more than giving them a quasi-jurisdictional nature, it would turn human rights commissions into organs of judicial control.[15] Even if this initiative has not moved forward, there are several measures that could improve the efficacy and level of compliance with the recommendations issued by these institutions, which could also contribute to the fulfillment of their role under international human rights law in accordance with the resolution of the UN General Assembly.

One of the measures that could possibly have a profound impact in human rights protection is the practice of 'awarding' reparations for the human rights violations and damages suffered by the direct and indirect victims. In addition to specific sections related to the facts and evidence presented by the parties, most of the recommendations currently issued have sections describing the legal situation and the observations and legal analysis of the facts that originated the claim. Of course, the commission issues the recommendations it deems prudent once it has analyzed the facts and pondered the evidence provided; however, it is at this precise procedural stage where it can recommend that the authority repairs the damages inflicted upon the victims, and thus determine the form and amount of the reparations to be provided.

One of the main obstacles for the protection of human rights is the lack of, or deficient, knowledge of this field, which finds an echo not only in the performance of authorities, but also in the recommendations issued by NHRIs. This lack of clarity is obviously not limited to an academic

---

(2011) 7 *Revista Separata del Periódico Oficial del Estado de Nuevo León* 7, 20, where he mentions that up to that moment, the work of the national human rights system of Mexico had focused on the social stigmatization of public institutions, without providing other means to achieve a more effective protection of human rights.

15 On the dangers of NHRIs issuing binding resolutions, see J. MADRAZO CUÉLLAR, 'Retos y Perspectivas del Sistema Nacional de Protección no Jurisdiccional de los Derechos Humanos' (1995) 12 *Derechos Humanos. Órgano Informativo de la Comisión de Derechos Humanos del Estado de México* 231, 240. The author considers that the objective of determining that an authority was responsible of a human rights violation is for it to perform a self-assessment, in order to convince itself that the violation could have been prevented, and thus to voluntarily comply with the recommendation, repair the damages and punish the perpetrators.

understanding of the issues at stake, but also to the direct applicability of international human rights law at the domestic level, constituting an obstacle for the promotion and effective protection of human rights. Therefore, an essential element that must be taken into consideration is one of the main objectives of international human rights law: the right to obtain reparation for damages. In many occasions, the State may have some notions on the issue of reparations, particularly from a civil law perspective. However, the situation is particularly different if seen from a human rights perspective, given that reparations do not consist exclusively of compensation but rather rely on several other bases such as guarantees of non-repetition and other complementary measures, which altogether seek to provide integral reparation.[16]

The purpose of including prospective reparations in the recommendations issued by human rights commissions is that the State has a clear view of the actions it must undertake to repair the damage inflicted in a given case, as well as of other measures that may be useful to avoid the repetition of a human rights violation. Thus, a recommendation may serve as a guideline for the State, and indicate in an objective and concise manner the type of reparation it would have to provide under a human rights approach. By having a clear image of the effects that a human rights violation produce on the State (either in its image or in the financial repercussions it may face), it may become more aware of its behavior and modify the circumstances that enable patterns of human rights violations to perpetuate within its structure. Certainly, these actions require the political and economic will of the government that has been deemed responsible; however, this may be an element that leads the authorities to form their own conviction on the need to comply with human rights standards, in order to contribute to the strengthening of the rule of law and to a legitimization of its actions before society.

---

16 It is important to mention how pertinent it is that NHRIs use the *Basic Principles and Guidelines on the Right to a Remedy and Reparation for Victims of Gross Violations of International Human Rights Law and Serious Violations of International Humanitarian Law*, in order to have a broader view of how they can contribute to the promotion and protection of human rights. General Assembly, *Basic Principles and Guidelines on the Right to a Remedy and Reparation for Victims of Gross Violations of International Human Rights Law and Serious Violations of International Humanitarian Law*, A/RES/60/147 (16 December 2005).

Another perspective that may be used by human rights commissions in Mexico, and which would help to standardize their performance at the national level, are the normative sources to their work. In this sense, the constitutional reform on human rights of 2011 has granted constitutional status to international human rights law in the country, which should be the parameter to guide the conduct and actions of these non-jurisdictional bodies. The use of international human rights law by the commissions would allow for the adoption of uniform standards and for the internalization of international law, granting more legal certainty to a field that in practical terms has just entered the domestic level.

If human rights commissions undertake their activities and legal consideration of claims brought before them from a standpoint based on international law, it will be more feasible that the recommendations they issue will have a broader view of human rights than those issued before the constitutional reform of 2011. Even if it is necessary for those standards to be considered in full knowledge and understanding of the situation in the country, this does not exclude that their use may provide a more protective perspective to the victims of human rights violations, given their greater level of development and the existence of tools and elements conceived under a human rights perspective.

Conversely, it is highly important for human rights commissions to use the recent criteria and developments under international law, regardless of their status as hard law or soft law. This is the more relevant when we consider that the resolutions adopted by multilateral organizations such as the UN, OECD, ILO or the OAS, even if not necessarily binding, do tend to provide a glimpse on the direction that international human rights law is moving, and on the situations that States will have to face in the near future. Additionally, the lack of a binding character at the international level doesn't necessarily mean that a standard will be equally soft under domestic law. As it has been the case with several human rights (like the right to water[17] or other economic, social and cultural rights), the recognition of their existence as an international right is sufficient evidence

17 See L.F. TELLO MORENO, 'Contribución de los organismos no jurisdiccionales de protección de los derechos humanos en el fortalecimiento del Estado de derecho: el caso del derecho al agua' (2010) 15 *Derechos Humanos México. Revista del Centro Nacional de los Derechos Humanos* 41, where the author mentions that the recommendations issued by human rights commissions on the right to safe-

for States to assess the feasibility of their protection and safeguard within their territorial boundaries. Furthermore, the existence of international guidelines or principles (that is, soft law norms) generally imply a lack of international political consensus, which is not an impediment for States to develop in their domestic spheres some specific characteristics of international law that may be of their interest.

In light of the silence of international law on the binding character of some rights, States can use their discretion to develop international human rights law within the domestic legal order. By virtue of this, human rights commissions play a preponderant role, given that their use of principles recognized in multilateral organizations can lead to important international and national developments, putting into practice the 'soft' rights that States may have been unable to elevate to the status of binding international norms.

Taking advantage of their position and recognition at the United Nations, as well as of their growing participation and role, national human rights institutions can become sufficient and important vehicles to achieve changes at the domestic, regional and international levels. They may therefore make a double use of international law: rely on international human rights law as a cohesive element that standardizes their performance, criteria, activities and assessment at the domestic level, while also helping through their actions, interpretation and domestic application of international law (through their recommendations and reports) to the development of binding and non-binding norms of international law. This may in turn contribute directly to the development of practice and norms in the international sphere.

V. CONCLUSION

National human rights institutions have before them the challenge of monitoring, from a human rights perspective, the performance and actions of the organs of the State. On the other hand, they have a mandate to contribute to the promotion of human rights at the domestic level, in

drinking water contribute to the strengthening of the national and international rule of law.

order to protect them and serve as a liaison between the government and its population, and between domestic and international law. Only an efficient, impartial and open position that takes into consideration the needs of the victims of human rights violations will be able to comply thoroughly with the mandate established by the Paris Principles and by the corresponding domestic (constitutional or legislative) framework. NHRIs must be considered as a mechanism that contributes to the monitoring of the respect of the international obligations undertaken by the State, while also acting as a bridge that enables the rebuilding of trust between the population, the government and the rule of law.

NOTES ON THE CONTRIBUTORS

Humberto Cantú Rivera is an Associate Researcher on human rights and Ph.D. Candidate at the Centre de recherche sur les droits de l'homme et le droit humanitaire (CRDH) of Panthéon-Assas University (Paris II). He has been a Visiting Professional at the Special Procedures Branch of the Office of the High Commissioner for Human Rights, and a Scholar of The Hague Academy of International Law. His research focuses on business and human rights, transitional justice, enforced disappearance, and economic, social and cultural rights.

Emmanuel Decaux is a Professor of Law at Panthéon-Assas University (Paris II) and the President of the UN Committee on Enforced Disappearances. He is currently the Director of the Doctoral School on International Law of Panthéon-Assas University (Paris II), where he also was the Director of the Centre de recherche sur les droits de l'homme et le droit humanitaire (CRDH). He has had an important career at the international level, where he served as a Member of the UN Sub-Commission for the Promotion and Protection of Human Rights and of the Advisory Committee to the Human Rights Council.

Navanethem Pillay is the former UN High Commissioner for Human Rights (2008–2014). She has also had a storied career in international criminal law, having served as Judge of the International Criminal Court and of the International Criminal Tribunal for Rwanda.

Olivier De Schutter is a Member of the UN Committee on Economic, Social and Cultural Rights, and was the UN Special Rapporteur on the right to food (2008–2014). He is a Professor of Law at the Université Catholique de Louvain, and has been a Visiting Professor for Columbia University.

Catarina de Albuquerque was the UN Special Rapporteur on the right to safe drinking water and sanitation (2008–2014). She led the discussion for the adoption of the Optional Protocol to the International Covenant on Economic, Social and Cultural Rights. She has also been a Visiting Professor at the University of Coimbra and Washington College of Law of American University.

John H. Knox is the first UN Special Rapporteur (and was the first Independent Expert) on human rights and the environment, and is the Henry C. Lauerman Professor of International Law at the School of Law of Wake Forest University.

Michael K. Addo is the Chair-Rapporteur of the UN Working Group on human rights and transnational corporations and other business enterprises, and is a Professor of Law at the University of Exeter.

Olivier de Frouville is a Member of the UN Human Rights Committee, and was a Member of the UN Working Group on enforced or involuntary disappearances, of which he was its Chair-Rapporteur between 2012–2013. He is a Professor of Law at Panthéon-Assas University (Paris II), and the Director of the Centre de recherche sur les droits de l'homme et le droit humanitaire (CRDH).

Magdalena Sepúlveda Carmona was the UN Special Rapporteur on extreme poverty and human rights (2008–2014), and currently works as a Senior Research Fellow at the UN Research Institute for Social Development.

Catalina Rivera Díaz is the First General Attorney on Human Rights of the Human Rights Commission of Nuevo Leon, in Monterrey, Mexico. She has been a Professor of Law for the School of Law and Criminology of Universidad Autonoma de Nuevo Leon for more than 20 years, and has been a Senior Legal Adviser for the State Women's Institute of Nuevo Leon. She was a shortlisted candidate for a position as Member of the UN Working Group on the issue on human rights and transnational corporations and other business enterprises.

Minerva Martínez Garza is the President of the Human Rights Commission of Nuevo Leon, in Monterrey, Mexico. She is a Professor of Law for the School of Law and Criminology of Universidad Autonoma de Nuevo Leon, in Monterrey, Mexico.

www.ingramcontent.com/pod-product-compliance
Ingram Content Group UK Ltd.
Pitfield, Milton Keynes, MK11 3LW, UK
UKHW021843100926
8556IPUK00019B/1023

9 781780 683447